THE NARRATIVE OF ARTHUR GORDON PYM

and the Abyss of Interpretation

TWAYNE'S MASTERWORK STUDIES

Robert Lecker, General Editor

THE NARRATIVE OF
ARTHUR GORDON PYM

and the Abyss of Interpretation

J. Gerald Kennedy

TWAYNE PUBLISHERS • NEW YORK
Maxwell Macmillan Canada • *Toronto*
Maxwell Macmillan International • *New York Oxford Singapore Sydney*

Twayne's Masterwork Series No. 135

The Narrative of Arthur Gordon Pym and the Abyss of Interpretation
J. Gerald Kennedy

Twayne Publishers   Maxwell Macmillan Canada, Inc.
Macmillan Publishing Company   1200 Eglinton Avenue East
866 Third Avenue   Suite 200
New York, New York 10022   Don Mills, Ontario M3C 3N1

Library of Congress Cataloging-in-Publication Data

Kennedy, J. Gerald.
    The narrative of Arthur Gordon Pym : and the abyss of interpretation / by
J. Gerald Kennedy.
        p.   cm.—(Twayne's masterwork studies ; no. 135)
    Includes bibliographical references and index.
    ISBN 0-8057-4455-X (cloth).—ISBN 0-8057-9443-3 (ppr)
    1. Poe, Edgar Allan, 1809–1849. Narrative of Arthur Gordon Pym.
I. Title. II. Series.
PS2618.N33K46   1994
813'.3—dc20   94-3667
                                                                    CIP

The paper used in this publication meets the minimum requirements of American
National Standard for Information Sciences—Permanence of Paper for Printed Library
Materials. ANSI Z3948–1984. ∞ ™

10 9 8 7 6 5 4 3 2 1 (hc)
10 9 8 7 6 5 4 3 2 1 (pb)

Printed in the United States of America

Contents

EDGAR ALLAN POE, 1848

Note on the References and Acknowledgments

The standard scholarly edition of *The Narrative of Arthur Gordon Pym* by Burton R. Pollin appears in the volume *The Imaginary Voyages*, volume 1, published by Twayne Publishers in 1981. Pollin's copious, informative notes and meticulous editing make this text essential to any serious study of Poe's novel. In my subsequent discussion of *Pym*, parenthetical page references are to this edition. My own annotated paperback edition of the novel and related tales is now available in the Oxford University Press World's Classics series, published in 1994.

I wish to express my special thanks to Richard Kopley for sharing with me the page proofs for his edited collection of essays, *Poe's "Pym": Critical Explorations*, published by Duke University Press in 1992. In preparing this volume I also received valuable assistance from Scott Peeples, Rob Hale, and Kirk Curnutt. Sarah Liggett Kennedy offered gentle encouragement and help with proofreading.

Chronology:
Edgar Allan Poe's Life and Works

1809	Edgar Allan Poe born 19 January in Boston to David Poe and Elizabeth Arnold Poe, itinerant actors.
1811	Father disappears and is presumed dead; mother dies in Richmond, Virginia, on 8 December, of a lingering pulmonary illness. Older brother, William Henry, goes to live with relatives in Baltimore; infant sister Rosalie is taken in by the Mackenzie family of Richmond. Nearly three years old, Edgar becomes the ward of Richmond merchant John Allan and his wife, Frances. Allan declines formal adoption.
1815	Sails with the Allan family in midsummer from Norfolk to Liverpool, England. Five weeks aboard the *Lothair* give him his earliest impressions of ocean voyaging. Asks his foster father to report him "not afraid coming across the Sea" (to Charles Ellis, 21 September 1815).
1815–1820	Lives with his foster parents in London, where Allan has established a branch office of his mercantile firm. Poe attends boarding schools in London and Stoke Newington.
1820	After financial reverses, Allan and family return to America, sailing aboard the *Martha* from Liverpool to New York for five weeks in June and July.
1820–1826	Attends Richmond schools, where he excels in Latin and French and in swimming, running, and jumping. Begins to write poetry.
1824	Mourns the death of Jane Stith Craig Stanard, the mother of his friend Robert Stanard, and visits her grave frequently. Marches with an honor guard during the visit of the Marquis

de Lafayette. Allan complains that Poe has become "miserable, sulky, and ill-tempered" (to Henry Poe, 1 November 1824) and seems ungrateful for Allan's care.

1825   Romance with Sarah Elmira Royster of Richmond.

1826   Enters the University of Virginia, where he earns excellent grades in Latin and French, but Poe's gambling debts and drinking cause Allan to curtail financial support. Poe withdraws from school, returns to Richmond, and learns of Sarah Royster's engagement to an older man.

1827   Following a major clash with Allan, leaves home and enlists in the army in Boston. There he publishes a chapbook, *Tamerlane and Other Poems*. Regiment transferred to South Carolina; en route to Charleston aboard the brig *Waltham*, Poe narrowly escapes shipwreck off Cape Cod.

1828   After 11 months at Fort Moultrie, Poe's battery is transferred to Fortress Monroe, Virginia. Andrew Jackson elected seventh president of the United States.

1829   Foster mother Frances Allan dies 28 February. With Allan's help, Poe hires a replacement to fill his military position, receiving official discharge 15 April. Moves to Baltimore and offers poems to various publishers. *Al Aaraaf, Tamerlane, and Minor Poems* appears before year's end in Baltimore under the imprint of Hatch & Dunning.

1830   Through Allan's intervention, is appointed cadet at West Point. Allan remarries. Poe indulges in "extreme dissipation," neglecting studies and military duties apparently in reaction to "humiliating privations" imposed by Allan (Poe to John Allan, 3 January 1831).

1831   Court-martial finds Poe guilty of "gross neglect of duty" and dismisses him from West Point. Thanks to advance orders by many cadets, publishes *Poems*, a new volume of poetry, under the imprint of Elam Bliss in New York. Moves to Baltimore in April and resides at the home of his grandmother Poe, joining aunt Maria Clemm; cousin Virginia; and brother William Henry Leonard Poe, himself a poet. Brother dies 1 August of "intemperance." Poe begins to write tales for a contest sponsored by the *Philadelphia Saturday Courier*.

1832   Loses contest, but the *Courier* publishes five of his mainly satirical tales. Submits stories to other journals and newspapers. In failing health, Allan drafts a new will that contains no provision for Poe. Andrew Jackson reelected president.

1833	Lives with aunt and cousin in Baltimore. Continues his parodies and imitations of popular fictional forms, now grouped as *Tales of the Folio Club*. Enters and wins contest for best tale with "Ms. Found in a Bottle," which appears in the *Baltimore Saturday Visiter*. Befriended by novelist John Pendleton Kennedy.
1834	Visits Allan, who rebuffs him. Allan dies 27 March in Richmond. Poe enlists Kennedy's help to find a publisher for 11 *Folio Club* tales.
1835	Kennedy encourages Poe to contact Thomas W. White, who has recently founded the *Southern Literary Messenger* in Richmond. The *Messenger* publishes several of Poe's reviews and tales, including "Berenice—A Tale" and "Hans Pfaall—A Tale." Poe returns to Richmond in August, taking an editorial position under White. Writes to Maria Clemm, proposing marriage to her daughter Virginia, and returns to Baltimore in September, possibly for a secret wedding ceremony. Mrs. Clemm and Virginia join Poe in Richmond in October.
1836	Proclaims himself editor of the *Messenger* and boosts circulation (though less than he claimed) through self-puffery, sarcastic reviews, and improved literary fare. Publishes articles on "Autography" and "Maelzel's Chess-Player." Publicly exchanges marriage vows with 13-year-old Virginia Clemm on 16 May. Harper and Brothers decline to publish the *Folio Club* tales, advising Poe that "readers in this country" prefer a "single and connected story" of book length (Harper and Brothers to Poe, June 1836). Poe publishes an essay-review on South Sea exploration and begins an extended sea narrative using the persona of Arthur Gordon Pym. White dismisses his employee at year's end, disgusted by Poe's peremptory manner and indiscreet drinking.
1837	Martin Van Buren inaugurated as president. January issue of the *Messenger* announces that Poe has "retired" from his editorial station, but includes the first installment of "The Narrative of Arthur Gordon Pym," as well as a lengthy review by Poe of Jeremiah N. Reynolds's *Expedition to the Pacific Ocean and South Seas*. Poe and family move to New York, where he completes his novel. Harper and Brothers announce the book in May, but a bank panic delays publication as a depression grips the country.
1838	Poe moves to Philadelphia with Virginia and her mother. Harper and Brothers issue *Pym* in late July, as the Wilkes

Expedition prepares to depart for the South Seas. Poe writes "Ligeia" and cultivates literary contacts in Philadelphia and Baltimore after 18 months of virtual inactivity as a magazinist.

1839   Assumes coeditorship of William Burton's *Gentleman's Magazine* in Philadelphia. Calls *Pym* "a silly book" in a letter to his new employer, who had reviewed it harshly. Begins a productive phase with "The Fall of the House of Usher" and more slashing reviews. Writes pieces on cryptography for *Alexander's Weekly Messenger*. Lea and Blanchard publish his collected *Tales of the Grotesque and Arabesque* in December.

1840   Publishes another travel hoax, "The Journal of Julius Rodman," in the *Gentleman's Magazine*. Accuses the poet Henry Wadsworth Longfellow of plagiarizing "Midnight Mass for the Dying Year" from Tennyson. Circulates a prospectus for his own journal, the *Penn Magazine*, which prompts Burton to fire him on 30 May. Poe enlists subscribers and contributors to the *Penn*, but "severe illness" (Poe to L. J. Cist, 30 December 1840) postpones first issue.

1841   John Tyler inaugurated as president. A bank panic further postpones publication of the *Penn*. Poe takes an editorial position at *Graham's Magazine* in February. Contributes reviews, cryptographic features, and tales, including "The Murders in the Rue Morgue." Solicits work for *Graham's* from Washington Irving, James Fenimore Cooper, William Cullen Bryant, Longfellow, and others. Unsuccessfully seeks government appointment from the Tyler administration; does not succeed. Meets anthologist and editor Rufus Griswold. Creates stir with new "Autography" series, which analyzes signatures of American authors.

1842   Virginia Poe suffers pulmonary hemorrhage; Poe indulges in intemperate drinking. Interviews Charles Dickens, on tour in America. Resigns from editorial staff of *Graham's*. Makes further efforts to obtain government appointment. Intoxicated, seeks employment in New York from editors of two periodicals. James Russell Lowell solicits Poe's work for his journal *Pioneer*.

1843   Lowell's journal publishes Poe's "The Tell-Tale Heart." Poe revives plans for his own magazine, to be called the *Stylus*. Visits Washington to seek position as collector of customs; goes on another alcoholic binge. Wins $100 prize from the *Dollar Newspaper* for "The Gold-Bug." Postpones publication of the *Stylus* because of financial problems. *The Doom of the Drinker*, a temperance novel by Thomas Dunn English, satirizes Poe's inebriation. Poe offers public lectures on American poetry.

1844 Moves to New York with Virginia and Mrs. Clemm, where he creates a sensation with "The Balloon-Hoax." Joins the staff of the *Evening Mirror*. Publishes "The Purloined Letter" in a popular gift book.

1845 Publishes his most popular poem, "The Raven," in the *Evening Mirror*. Lectures on poetry and achieves celebrity status within New York literary circles; becomes friendly with poet Frances S. Osgood. Poe is hired by Charles F. Briggs to coedit the *Broadway Journal*. Again attacks Longfellow as a plagiarist. Becomes "editor and proprietor" of the *Broadway Journal* in July. Wiley and Putnam publish a new volume of Poe's *Tales* and a collection called *The Raven and Other Poems*. Poe scandalizes a Boston audience by reading his early "Al Aaraaf" instead of a new poem.

1846 The *Broadway Journal* folds on 3 January. Having impugned the reputation of Mrs. E. F. Ellett, a New York poet, Poe scuffles with her defender, Thomas Dunn English. *Graham's Magazine* publishes Poe's "Philosophy of Composition." Poe begins his controversial series, "The Literati of New York," in *Godey's Lady's Book*. Moves with his family to a cottage in Fordham (now part of the Bronx), where Virginia suffers from advanced tuberculosis and his own health weakens. Becomes a frequent target of magazine satire and parody. *Godey's* publishes "The Cask of Amontillado." Poe and Virginia are "dangerously ill" (*New York Morning Express*, 15 December 1846) and destitute.

1847 Virginia dies 30 January; Poe continues to suffer a serious illness. Wins libel suit against the editors of the *Evening Mirror*. The *American Review* publishes "Ulalume—a Ballad."

1848 Composes a cosmological lecture, published in expanded form in July as the prose poem *Eureka*. Meets Mrs. Annie Richmond in Lowell, Massachusetts. Poe enters into a literary romance with Sarah Helen Whitman of Providence. Visits Annie in the fall, proposes marriage to Sarah, and stages a suicide attempt when Mrs. Whitman's family opposes the union. Poe writes "For Annie," and delivers lectures based on his essay "The Poetic Principle." Revives his project to publish the *Stylus*.

1849   Publishes a last flurry of poems and tales, including "Hop-Frog." Entertains an unlikely scheme to publish the *Stylus* in Oquawka, Illinois. Returns to Richmond and renews his romance with widow Sarah Elmira Royster Shelton, whom he had courted in 1825. Poe delivers lectures and gives poetry readings in Virginia. Collapses near a polling place in Baltimore, probably of a cerebral hemorrhage induced by alcoholic excess. Dies 7 October in Washington Hospital, reportedly calling for "Reynolds." Reputation sullied by Rufus Griswold's vicious obituary profile.

LITERARY AND
HISTORICAL CONTEXT

1

The Cultural Foreground of the 1830s

Poe composed his only novel, *The Narrative of Arthur Gordon Pym*, as Andrew Jackson passed the reins of government to his chosen successor, Martin Van Buren. In the eight years of Jackson's presidency (1829–37), the young republic had undergone a dramatic transformation, embracing the democratic populism championed by Jackson, who personified the backwoods, self-made man. The former Indian fighter enjoyed a good scrap and wielded political power by appealing to the common people rather than to an intellectual elite. During his two terms, electoral politics changed irreversibly as the old caucus system, controlled by the educated and privileged few, gave way to a more open process based on the popular vote. The fiercely contested election of 1828 first pitted Democrats against National Republicans, giving rise to the party system as it encouraged partisan journalism and open castigation of political rivals.

But heated factional battles over banking and monetary reforms, protective tariffs, and internal improvements betrayed deeper, more ominous divisions in the body politic. Behind the wrangling over the construction of roads, canals, and railroads vital to the opening of the American heartland lay the larger issue of whether the states or the national government should oversee such development. Likewise, Jackson's war with Nicholas Biddle and the National Bank hinged on whether a central bank ought to control the country's economy, or whether such consolidation served the interests of the wealthy and discriminated against state banks and ordinary citizens. The tariff question most fully exposed the underlying issue of states' rights: the manufacturing interests of the North wanted heavy import duties that were unpopular in the South and West, where there was greater dependence on European goods. Although Jackson reluctantly accepted the need for protective duties, John C. Calhoun, his vice president, insisted that states possessed a constitutional right to nullify adverse federal laws and even to secede from the United States if the national government attempted to force compliance. The legislature of South Carolina (the home state of both Jackson and Calhoun) passed just such an ordinance in 1832. Although a compromise on the tariff question seemed to resolve the nullification controversy in 1833, the episode revealed the increasingly precarious nature of the Union and the rancorous mistrust between advocates of states' rights and those defending the supremacy of the federal government.

The battle over tariffs, which caused an acrimonious break between Jackson and Calhoun, disclosed yet another insidious problem. What troubled voters in South Carolina more than import duties was the implicit threat to the institution of slavery, which supported the agricultural economy of the South. Slavery had long been outlawed in Northern states, the Missouri Compromise (1820) had limited its spread in the Louisiana Territory, and now abolitionists were launching a campaign to eliminate all slavery in the United States. In 1831 William Lloyd Garrison began to publish his provocative newspaper, the *Liberator*, and eight months later the bloody Nat Turner Rebellion in Virginia terrified Southerners and dramatized for them the danger of exciting slaves with the idea of freedom. Many Southerners reasoned that if Northern politicians could conspire to impose a tariff bill hostile to Southern interests, they might also manage to impose abolition unless the South defended the sovereignty of individual states and the primacy of property rights in a federal system of government. By threatening secession, South Carolina raised the specter of a nation divided over the intertwined issues of slavery, states' rights, and national union.

Through deft negotiation, Jackson worked out a compromise on the nullification crisis that produced a long moratorium on talk of Southern secession. But the issue of slavery remained an ongoing controversy, erupting every time a new state joined the Union. The American Antislavery Society formed in 1833 a powerful new coalition for abolition, prompting an increasing stridency and defensiveness in the South. Racial tensions ran high in the North as well, and bloody race riots erupted in 1835 in Philadelphia and Washington. Emboldened by the crusade for abolition, African-Americans manifested their hatred of slavery more openly than before, while various white groups resorted to violence to demonstrate their resistance to social change. Several Southern states indignantly outlawed the circulation of abolitionist tracts and punished agitators. In this climate of hostility, Poe edited and published an unsigned review in the *Southern Literary Messenger* of April 1836, presumably by his friend Judge Beverley Tucker, defending the "much abused" practice of slavery as the basis of "all our institutions." This piece extolled the concept of private property and idealized the "moral feelings" engendered by the master-slave relationship, imputing an innate dependency to the "Negro." Some scholars have argued that Poe wrote the review himself; whether or not he embraced its fundamental assumptions about race, he knew that such pronouncements would gratify Southern readers who supported the Richmond journal.

For all the vehemence with which Poe's contemporaries debated abolition and property rights, no one could quite foresee the cataclysmic results of the rift between the North and South that widened in the mid-1830s. While the slavery issue simmered, many other campaigns and projects commanded public attention. During the thirties, the federal government engaged in a long and cruel operation to force five major Indian tribes to leave their ancestral grounds and resettle west of the Mississippi. The so-called Removal Act of 1830 led to a drawn-out war in Florida between army troops and the Seminoles under Chief Osceola; in Georgia, soldiers rounded up Cherokees by the thousands, destroyed their homes, and shipped them down a "trail of tears" to a newly designated Indian territory. Jackson coerced dozens of other tribes into signing treaties that entailed "voluntary" displacement to the West, all in an effort to avoid further Indian reprisals for the relentless incursion of white settlers.

Indeed, the westward movement of pioneers continued unabated during the 1830s. Arkansas and Michigan entered the Union, and Iowa and Wisconsin became formally organized as territories. While United States troops pushed Native Americans beyond the Mississippi, the government annexed more and more land west of the river, thus reducing the buffer zone that the Removal Act had been designed to create. Meanwhile, railroad building increased dramatically in the thirties, promoting trade and resettlement in the West, where markets were opening up. Expeditions led by Captain Benjamin Bonneville, Joseph Walker, and Nathaniel Wyeth in the years 1832–35 helped to open up the Rocky Mountains, California, and the Pacific Northwest, respectively, for settlement and commerce. Trailblazers such as these men captured the popular imagination, inspiring such works as Washington Irving's *The Adventures of Captain Bonneville* (1837) and Poe's fictional "The Journal of Julius Rodman" (1840). Westward expansion provoked discussion about the extension of slavery but to some extent also distracted the nation from regional concerns with its promise of land and opportunity.

While pioneers continued to pour into the "Great West," however, American cities grew rapidly. Between 1820 and 1840, the urban population nearly doubled, and the ports of the East—Boston, New York, Philadelphia, and Baltimore—began to resemble the manufacturing cities of Europe both in commercial bustle and in the wretchedness, filth, and overcrowding associated with industrialization. River towns such as Cincinnati, Louisville, and New Orleans also acquired urban characteristics, thanks to trade facilitated by steamboats plying the Ohio and the Mississippi rivers. As these cities contended with the emerging problems of sanitation and crime, they became centers of a nascent mass culture created by the newspapers and magazines that proliferated after the introduction of steam-powered printing in 1827. This boom in periodical publishing created a market for popular fiction, specifically short stories and serialized novels.

The Cultural Foreground of the 1830s

It would be hard to overestimate the impact of this last development on the shaping of American literature. The new weekly and monthly magazines encouraged literally hundreds of aspiring authors to bring their literary wares before the public. At a time when U.S. publishing houses regularly "pirated" and sold—at great profit—unauthorized editions of novels by popular British authors (there being no international copyright law), American writers faced huge disadvantages in the book trade. Periodicals such as *Godey's Lady's Book* (1830), the *New England Magazine* (1831), the *Knickerbocker* (1833), the *American Monthly Magazine* (1833), the *Southern Literary Messenger* (1834), the *Southern Literary Journal* (1835), the *United States Magazine and Democratic Review* (1837), and Burton's *Gentleman's Magazine* (1837) spurred American writing, however, with contests offering premiums for new poetry, fiction, and essays; with fixed rates for original submissions; with editorial puffery stirring interest in featured authors; and with growing subscription lists that made periodical writing a desired commodity. In a very real sense, these magazines helped to construct the public notion of what American literature was about—and where it was going.

For several established American authors, the decade brought new challenges to their reputations: Irving, who had returned to the United States in 1832 after a lengthy stay in Europe, tried to regain his standing as a native author with an excursion along the frontier that led to a string of Western narratives displaying his commitment to American themes and contemporary materials. In addition to his account of Captain Bonneville, Irving penned *A Tour of the Prairies* (1835) and *Astoria* (1837). William Cullen Bryant, the celebrated poet, used his position as editor of the *New York Evening Post* to advance his own Democratic, abolitionist, and prolabor views, but he also delivered sharp literary judgments on his contemporaries and used the newspaper's pages to feature his own narratives of the frontier. In such writing, he followed the model of James Fenimore Cooper, who had himself returned from a sojourn in Europe in 1833, and who (like Irving) immediately faced the problem of reestablishing himself as an American author. But the more combative Cooper instead launched an attack on his critics in *A Letter to His Countrymen* (1834), and in

Homeward Bound (1838) and *Home as Found* (1838) he aroused ire by contrasting cosmopolitan types with American boors and dolts. While Catherine Maria Sedgwick, author of the novel *Hope Leslie* (1827), enjoyed continuing popularity through tales of frontier life appearing in the *Token* (an annual or "gift book"), the *Gift* (another annual), and *Godey's*, Lydia Maria Child (whose 1824 novel *Hobomok* had inspired Cooper) nearly destroyed her literary reputation with her uncompromising abolitionist manifesto, *An Appeal in Favor of That Class of Americans Called Africans* (1833).

Meanwhile, new authors began to forge significant careers in the 1830s. Early in the decade Nathaniel Hawthorne published anonymous tales in the *Salem Gazette*, the *Token*, and the *New England Magazine*, recasting scenes from New England history as ambiguous moral fables. Finally acknowledging his authorship, he published his first collection, *Twice-Told Tales*, in 1837. In 1835 Poe became a regular contributor to the *Southern Literary Messenger*, where as acting editor he published many of his own Gothic and burlesque tales; after a brief hiatus he returned to the magazine world in 1838 at the helm of Burton's *Gentleman's Magazine*. Ralph Waldo Emerson renounced his position as a clergyman in 1832 and soon launched his career as a Transcendentalist lecturer and essayist, bringing out his influential monograph *Nature* (1836). William Gilmore Simms, who penned the border romance *The Yemassee* (1835), published historical narratives in the *Southern Literary Journal*, and toward the end of the decade, Harriet Beecher Stowe began contributing frequent tales to *Godey's*. Finally, as a point of contrast to the incipient careers here cited, we may note that in 1838, Frederick Douglass (who in 1845 would publish his searing *Narrative of the Life of Frederick Douglass, An American Slave*) escaped from bondage in Maryland to find refuge in abolitionist New England.

As American literature became more diverse and democratic in tone, the broader culture also underwent significant changes with the growth of urban centers. The larger cities offered certain amenities rarely found in the provinces: theaters, art galleries, concert halls, well-stocked public libraries, museums, and public lectures. The lyceum movement, which swept the country in the 1830s, popularized high-toned civic discussion of art, literature, music, religion, philoso-phy, and various moral issues fueling the reform movements of the time (including those urging temperance and abolition). Equally popu-lar were lectures on various branches of science, including the natural sciences applied in continental and global exploration. The public craved "useful and entertaining knowledge" (as it was called in the magazine trade) and prized—even reverenced—factual information about lands and regions then scarcely known.

While the American West commanded great interest, one major focus of contemporary curiosity was the South Pacific and the polar region beyond. In the mid-1830s, the United States belatedly prepared to enter into Pacific exploration, which had long been dominated by the British, the French, and the Russians. Captain Jeremiah N. Reynolds, who had participated in a commercial and scientific voyage in the years 1829–30, collaborated with Captain Matthew Fontaine Maury to badger Congress into supporting a major exploration pro-ject. In June 1836 the Jackson administration appointed Captain Thomas ap Catesby Jones to head such an expedition, but wrangling over ways and means postponed the adventure; Jones resigned, and in August 1838 Commodore Charles Wilkes embarked with a modest fleet on a four-year voyage of discovery to the South Seas.

Poe's novel of polar adventure, delayed in publication by the bank panic of 1837, thus appeared in July 1838, just as the American expedition prepared to set out for that enticing yet ill-charted region. Read against the political turbulence and racial unrest of the Jackson years, *The Narrative of Arthur Gordon Pym* exploits contemporary aspirations and anxieties as it depicts a fantastic voyage culminating in death and revelation somewhere near the South Pole.

2

The Significance of *Pym*

American literature abounds with remarkable texts not perceived as classic until long after their composition. Herman Melville's *Moby-Dick* (1851) is one such neglected masterwork; Poe's novel *The Narrative of Arthur Gordon Pym* (1838) is another. Though not on the same scale of achievement as Melville's great novel, *Pym* bears comparison as a sea story insofar as it prefigures *Moby-Dick* in its representation of a world pervaded by deception, illusion, and violence; in its symbolic and even mythic structure; and in its exploration of the sublime terror associated with absolute whiteness. Narrated by young men who have survived initiations at sea, both novels depict voyages that begin in Nantucket and that proceed toward scenes of destruction in the South Seas; both combine prosaic documentation with depictions of fabulous exploits. Whether *Pym* had any direct influence on Melville's novel remains uncertain, but the parallels between the two books continue to provoke critical speculation.[1] Both authors seem to have drawn from a common source: the writing of Captain Jeremiah N. Reynolds. Poe borrowed details on South Sea exploration (especially in chapter 16 of his novel) from several writings by Reynolds, whose 1839 article on the white whale Mocha Dick is likewise thought to have influenced Melville.[2] Both *Pym* and *Moby-Dick* appeared, coincidentally, under the imprint of Harper and Brothers.

The two novels also shared the fate of prolonged neglect. Whereas critical appreciation of Melville's work developed belatedly in the 1920s, *Pym* has emerged as a novel of major significance only in the past 40 years. Shortly after its publication Poe himself dismissed it as "a very silly book," but as Burton R. Pollin has shown, contemporary reviewers generally credited its imaginative power even when they questioned its authenticity.[3] The novel enjoyed little commercial success in its day, however, and after appearing in two British editions (1838, 1841) it soon vanished from public view. In 1856 the novel was included in the Redfield edition of Poe's *The Complete Works* and for years remained available only in succeeding multivolume editions of Poe. Thanks to the French translation of Charles Baudelaire, *Pym* exercised notable influence on Jules Verne, who wrote a sequel titled *Le Sphinx des glaces* (The Sphinx of the Ice Fields, 1895), and on Arthur Rimbaud, who offered poetic homage in his *Bateau ivre* (The Drunken Boat, 1871). Ordinarily dismissive of Poe, even Henry James acknowledged in *The Golden Bowl* (1904) the great imagination displayed in *Pym*. But early biographers and critics generally gave the narrative only perfunctory attention. Finally, in a 1950 introduction to a collection of Poe's writings, the distinguished poet W. H. Auden characterized *Pym* as one of Poe's "most important works" and placed it among "the finest adventure stories ever written."[4] Whether Auden's endorsement triggered the modern discovery of *Pym* or merely anticipated its revaluation, the past four decades have witnessed a spectacular reversal of critical opinion, with the novel assuming a central position in most sustained discussions of Poe's achievement.

This prominence derives partly, as we shall see, from the critical climate of the late twentieth century, for *Pym* lends itself to an unusually wide array of readings. But the narrator's odyssey also carries rich, universal implications of its own, staging the rites of passage by which a young man throws off innocence and attains a bleak vision of human violence and treachery. We can now see that, for all its gory sensationalism, *Pym* raises provocative questions of epistemology and metaphysics. In its documentary phases, the narrative seems to assert the possibility of understanding the phenomenal world in some definite, empirical way. Geographic and scientific information appears to validate the truthfulness of the narrative as it demonstrates the intelligibility of physical reality. Yet the young narrator repeatedly makes faulty inferences by misreading visual signs. Recurrent instances of human deception—ruses, ploys, masquerades—parallel the contradictory relationship in the natural world between appearance and reality. Experience disconfirms Pym's assumptions so persistently that the very possibility of arriving at "truth" becomes doubtful and problematic. Because Poe inserts this critique of reason and judgment within a text that finally flaunts its own spurious nature—through an improbable ending and an accompanying note—the novel conveys a radical uncertainty; that is, *Pym* posits an analogy between the literary hoax and the deceptive "pasteboard mask" of the physical world (to appropriate a relevant phrase from *Moby-Dick*).

If Poe's novel sometimes betrays authorial carelessness in its so-called patchwork construction and its repackaging of documentary material, the narrative nevertheless includes many brilliant, unforgettable scenes that cohere to form a riveting tale of survival. Repeatedly Pym faces the threat of death; his story amounts to a compendium of such Poesque horrors as premature burial, murder, dismemberment, shipwreck, and massacre. These dire events unfold not as scenes of gratuitous violence but as stages in the apparent education of the narrator. Each episode discloses mythic or psychic dimensions that multiply the implications of Pym's journey and underscore its symbolic nature. But Poe also calls into question the understanding that his narrator supposedly acquires, leaving in doubt the possibility of education in a world of ubiquitous illusion. The final, ambiguous episode, in which Pym seems to disappear in a polar cataract, dramatizes either revelation or delirium; in either case, it betrays authorial mystification as Poe leaves his reader literally hanging on the edge of an interpretive abyss. The "shrouded human figure" rising up out of the vortex epitomizes the problem of meaning that pervades the novel.

For all its flaws (and we should recall the stylistic incongruities of *Moby-Dick*), *Pym* unfolds a powerful fable of the human need to interpret life-shaping events in relation to a transcendent meaning or purpose. The narrator's craving for certitude and his persistent efforts to construe his experience as fortune or misfortune reveal a seemingly naive faith in providence. Unlike Daniel Defoe's *Robinson Crusoe* (1719), the novel from which Poe learned the "potent magic of verisimilitude,"[5] *Pym* does not finally convey an unquestionable sense of divine benevolence; on the contrary, the narrator's supplications to the Creator typically presage scenes implying the perverseness of fate or the irrationality of experience. Pym's willingness to believe in a benign deity and an orderly world stands in stark contrast to the horrors that he undergoes. Yet for all these ironies, Pym survives—or seems to—through the apparent intervention of the white figure in the cataract; his salvation seems to justify his belief in a loving God. Has Pym been rescued by a heavenly form, though, or vaporized by an author racked by private frustrations? This is the enigma of *Pym* that haunts the reader, for the novel enacts the metaphysical crisis of modernity itself: the longing for faith before the great, silent void of nonbeing. Like certain other literary works, among them Franz Kafka's novel *The Trial* (1925), Poe's novel prefigures the spiritual dilemma that now conditions our reading of the protagonist's struggle against meaninglessness.

3

Critical Reception and Continuing Controversy

Poe began to compose a novel in late 1836 because he could not interest Harper and Brothers in a collection of separate tales; the publisher insisted that the reading public demanded a "single and connected story" of book length. Two installments of *Pym* appeared in the *Southern Literary Messenger* in early 1837, but Poe's dismissal from his post at the journal (and subsequent removal to New York) delayed his work on the novel even as it compounded his economic difficulties. There is considerable evidence to suggest Poe's hostility toward the popular audience that he was forced to placate. In the April 1836 issue of the *Messenger*, for example, he decried the "misapplied patriotism" that caught American readers in "the gross paradox of liking a stupid book the better, because, sure enough, its stupidity is American."[1] When compelled to write a novel-length narrative for this same audience, he seized on a topic of contemporary interest—exploration of the South Seas—and freely plagiarized extant accounts to give his story a ring of authenticity. He had expected the publication to coincide with the government expedition organized at the urging of nautical explorers Jeremiah N. Reynolds and Matthew Fontaine Maury. Yet administrative conflicts postponed the departure of the American ships, and the bank panic of 1837 delayed the publication of *Pym* for more than a year while its author languished in poverty.

After prompting an initial round of reviews that expressed vexation or grudging admiration, *Pym* disappeared, remaining in critical obscurity for decades. The only substantial interpretation to precede the modern rediscovery of the novel was Marie Bonaparte's provocative, explicitly Freudian analysis (first published in French in 1933) of the narrator's journey as a quest for the Mother, a search that culminates in the appearance of a maternal figure in the warm, milky waters of the polar region.[2] To be sure, a handful of scholarly essays from the thirties and forties also located the original sources of various plagiarized passages in *Pym*; these studies helped to clarify the historical context while supporting the notion of an uninspired author ransacking contemporary travel accounts to pad his tale and achieve the requisite commercial length. Literary historians have greatly expanded our knowledge of the novel's textual antecedents, its composition history, and its early reception while generally skirting its interpretive challenges.

The task of interpretation has been taken up only in the past 40 years, and without exaggeration it might be said that the shifts and turns in *Pym* criticism over four decades closely mirror the transformations of modern critical thought. Two years after W. H. Auden's 1950 declaration of the novel's importance, Patrick Quinn published a seminal essay, later incorporated in his book *The French Face of Edgar Poe* (1957), in which he suggested why French readers had long regarded *Pym* as one of Poe's "major accomplishments." Building his argument on the assumptions of the New Criticism, which approached the text as a structurally unified artifact, Quinn described a work "remarkably coherent in its management of structure and theme," and he outlined the novel's patterns of revolt and deception as well as its doppelgänger motif, thus revealing the psychological design that makes *Pym* the "crucial text" for gaining an understanding of Poe's methods.[3] Quinn's stunning revaluation had an obvious impact on Edward H. Davidson, who characterized the novel as "central to Poe's mind and thought" in *Poe: A Critical Study* (1957). Davidson examined the epistemological implications of deception and revolt, prompting his conclusion that all is illusion: "the mind makes its own reality." Nevertheless, he regarded the novel as a study of the "emergence and growth" of the "thinking self."[4] Similarly, Harry Levin, in *The Power of Blackness* (1958), focused on Pym's journey "to the end of night"—toward death—as a "material" (rather than a spiritual) narrative that defies theological interpretation; his thematic reading explored the racial implications of the Tsalal section but dismissed Poe's editorial note at the novel's end as a non sequitur that vitiates the concluding polar scene.[5]

Two important readings of *Pym* appeared in the 1960s, heralding a decade of increasing critical attention. In *Love and Death in the American Novel* (1966), Leslie Fiedler proposed *Pym* as "the archetypal American story," a precursor of *Moby-Dick* and Mark Twain's *The Adventures of Huckleberry Finn* (1884) in its "rejection of the family and the world of women" in favor of "pure male companionship." Imputing homoerotic tendencies to Pym, Fiedler endorsed Bonaparte's reading but claimed that the closing scene links the "Great Mother" to "total destruction, a death without resurrection." He also observed that as a "social document," *Pym* takes slavery as its subject; the narrator voyages toward a disguised version of the American South and so expresses Poe's racial fears.[6] A related perspective informed Sidney Kaplan's introduction to the 1960 Hill and Wang edition of *Pym*. Noting Poe's advocacy of slavery and his fictional caricatures of slaves (like Jupiter in "The Gold-Bug" [1843]), Kaplan saw the Tsalal episode as "an allegorical and didactic damning of the Negro," conveyed as an immutable, divine judgment on the race.[7]

Other essays from the 1960s, however, raised doubts about these subtle explications. In 1963 L. Moffitt Cecil challenged the idea of unity in *Pym* and described its two-part scheme.[8] Two years later, Walter E. Bezanson elaborated on the "dream recital" articulated by Quinn but challenged Davidson's thesis that the narrator moves toward understanding. He commented on Poe's fondness for a "surface game of credibility" while disputing the New Critical assumption of organic unity, insisting that *Pym* is "not a novel" but rather "three stories" linked by "flummery" and marred by discontinuities.[9]

Likewise, J. V. Ridgely and Iola S. Haverstick, who investigated the history of *Pym*'s composition, argued in 1966 that the narrative had been written in several stages by a distracted author and that it thus possesses only a "spurious unity." Countering the "subtle readings" of Quinn, Levin, Fiedler, and Kaplan, they claimed that "the story lacks a controlling theme and has no uncontrovertible serious meaning."[10] In 1967, continuing the wave of skeptical reactions to revisionary claims about *Pym*, Sidney P. Moss refined Cecil's argument to suggest that the narrative consists of two discrete stories that render thematic readings fallacious. Summarizing Poe's errors and inconsistencies, Moss accused Quinn, Davidson, and Fiedler of "impressionistic criticism" showing more ingenuity than insight.[11]

As American textual scholars and literary historians questioned the interpretive claims of the 1950s, the French critic Jean Ricardou raised doubts about the multiplication of hypotheses in thematic criticism. Exploring a passage on the strange waters of Tsalal, Ricardou in 1967 discerned a metaphor for writing and suggested that *Pym* portrays a "voyage to the end of the page." This analysis called attention to Poe's self-reflexive interest in the act of writing, to the hieroglyphic characters on Tsalal, and to the chasms resembling gigantic written characters. Ricardou claimed to offer a complete reading of the water passage even as he shifted discussion to a metatextual plane, construing the scenes on Tsalal as a "dramatization of the ink-paper antagonism" and the whiteness of the polar seas as a figure of the inevitable blank page at the end of an unfinished manuscript. In the interpretive model of Ricardou, *Pym* furnished a commentary on its own composition.[12]

Near the close of the decade, Joel Porte in *The Romance in America* (1969) discussed Poe's narrative as a deeply ironic quest for truth and revelation that leads toward "eternal terror." He regarded the narrator as a fool or a dupe whose need to believe in his own "sweet reasonableness" and in a "rational creator" causes him to miss the "dark inferences that Poe forces on the reader." Porte presented a fable of misreading in which Pym attempts "frantically and vainly" to reduce the "deep ambiguity in nature" to coherent meaning. The voyage itself leads toward "the beginning of consciousness and to that core of fear at the heart of the interior self."[13]

During the 1970s, as theory entered into American critical discourse and generated new interpretive strategies, studies of *Pym* became more numerous and diverse. In a 1971 thematic reading Joseph J. Moldenhauer argued that the death-haunted novel portrays a quest for self-destruction that mirrors Poe's sense of the creative process itself. Because Moldenhauer saw the entire adventure as a projection of Pym's perverse imagination—in which destruction and deliverance are identical—he read the concluding scene as an artistic realization of "perfect unity." Here the enigmatic ending corroborates perfectly Moldenhauer's New Critical assumption that a work of art by definition possesses formal and conceptual unity.[14] Critical willingness to read *Pym* as a coherent search for transcendence, spiritual redemption, or cosmic oneness—which may be said to date from Charles O'Donnell's 1962 essay[15]—informed several important essays of the early seventies. Perhaps the most engaging of these appeared in 1972 in Daniel Hoffman's provocative *Poe Poe Poe Poe Poe Poe Poe*. Hoffman framed a personal reading merging Freudian insights from Bonaparte and a perception (reminiscent of Davidson and Porte) of Pym's ironic status as a victim of self-deception. He saw the narrator as torn between reason and unreason—a split mirrored by his attachments to two alter egos, Augustus Barnard and Dirk Peters, respectively. Ultimately Pym's "regressive imagination" leads by novel's end, according to Hoffman, to the savage, intuitive self; to a death that is a rebirth; to "the realization of a supraconsciousness in the moment of the self's annihilation." Hoffman advanced a mythic reading as he concluded that Pym has entered "the womb of the world itself" to be "reborn."[16]

Four other critics reached roughly similar conclusions in 1973. In an elegant introduction to the Godine edition of *Pym*, Richard Wilbur conceded that the novel has "architectural deficiencies" but that it nevertheless forms a "coherent allegory" representing the narrator's "spiritual quest" as a dream experience. Through biblical glosses, Wilbur situated the story in an explicitly Christian framework; yet like Hoffman he interpreted Pym's voyage as a regressive movement in time toward the origins of his own being. For Wilbur, this motif of return to Tsalal represents the "curse" of Pym's birth, which he must reenact to reach that source of absolute light and life described in the novel's closing lines in "the language of homecoming."[17] Todd Lieber made a slightly different case in *Endless Experiments*, detailing the narrator's search for a "pure selfhood" ultimately achieved through "the redeeming power of the imagination."[18] In *Edgar Allan Poe: A Phenomenological View*, David Halliburton defined yet another kind of transformation; focusing on Pym's "three inhumations," he described a condition of "isolation and victimization" that precipitates the narrator's journey toward "a space beyond the word," toward "the great salvation."[19] In an essay the same year, meanwhile, Paul John Eakin focused on the paradox of communicating the incommunicable, reading *Pym* as a singular instance of Poe's "Lazarus plot": an attempt to gain forbidden knowledge through visionary experience followed by a return to the mundane. Eakin made the ingenious argument that the equivocal conclusion (in which Pym seems both to perish and to survive) reflects Poe's solution to the problem of how to experience real death but then to communicate its spiritual revelations.[20]

Against these various arguments for reading *Pym* as a serious, more or less unified representation of spiritual or psychic transformation—to which we might add the subsequent judgment in David Ketterer's 1979 *The Rationale of Deception in Poe*[21]—the 1970s witnessed a number of readings informed by a more skeptical view of the novel's unity and purpose. In the 1973 work *Poe's Fiction: Romantic Irony in the Gothic Tales*, G. R. Thompson invoked the tradition of German Romanticism to recast the argument of Edward Davidson, emphasizing the futility of human efforts to penetrate the world of illusion and arrive at some primal truth. Pointing to unexpected twists in Pym's account, Thompson read these ironic reversals as signs of the "deceptive perversity of fortune" and argued that *Pym* finally confirms Poe's view of man as "a forlorn, perverse sentient being buried alive in the incomprehensible tomb of the universe."[22] In a widely cited 1974 essay, Robert L. Carringer contended that the novel falters and collapses because the claustrophobic "circumscription of space"—that generative principle of Poe's best tales—proves inimical to the requirements of the long sea narrative. Carringer also exposed what he regarded as the dubious assumptions of "transcendental" readings of

Pym; that is, readings that see Poe's poetic quest for ideal beauty as carrying over into his fiction and anticipating the union of matter and spirit postulated in *Eureka*.[23] In a 1975 essay Claude Richard followed the metatextual approach of Ricardou, tracing Poe's concern with reading and writing throughout *Pym*. Richard unfolded in detail the narrator's attempt in chapter 5 to read a cryptic message from Augustus, arguing that at novel's end Pym must choose between Tsalal, "the domain of unreadable writing," and the polar region, which signifies the "end of writing."[24] In my 1976 article I emphasized the hoaxical aspect of *Pym* and found in Poe's supposed errors and inconsistencies authorial mockery of a naive reading public: the universe itself proves to be a hoax, a scheme of appearances that resists interpretation; Pym's attempt to decipher the warning from Augustus is a metaphor for the unreadability of the phenomenal world.[25] John Carlos Rowe in a 1977 essay similarly examined this last incident as a figure for "the doubleness of writing," the paradoxical fullness and emptiness implicit in its signifying function. Rowe's reading marked the first full-scale deconstruction of *Pym* along rigorously theoretical lines; in his view Poe's novel exposes the illusion that writing can "represent" truth. Moreover, Rowe concluded (as had Davidson, Porte, Thompson, and others) that Pym "remains blind to the metaphysical and spiritual implications of his adventure."[26]

By the late 1980s a new division in *Pym* criticism had thus developed between those disposed to view Pym's voyage as a meaningful journey toward illumination or redemption and those inclined to see it as a deeply ironic commentary on self-deception and misreading. Even as other essays of the decade reflected various methods and concerns, they tended to fall on one side or the other of this split. So, for example, William C. Spengemann discussed the conventions of travel narratives and literary hoaxes to clarify Poe's "subversive manipulations of narrative form." In Spengemann's view, *Pym* finally suggests that "the disordered psyche constitutes the only reality."[27] Two essays in the 1978 special number of *American Transcendental Quarterly*, which was devoted to *Pym*, deserve special notice. The facts adduced in Alexander Hammond's reconsideration of the book's composition (completed, he believed, in June 1837) supported the reading of *Pym* as "a self-referential novel ironically concerned with illusion and fiction-making."[28] Barton Levi St. Armand elucidated Jungian implications of Pym's various metamorphoses and traced the latter's approach toward "the Great Mother," but called his transformation incomplete, noting that Pym has "not yet learned how to read, how to decipher the runes of mythic reality."[29] In a 1978 study, however, Kent Ljungquist insisted on the "sublime evocation" of the final scene; he connected the gigantic white figure to the Titan myth and concluded that Pym at last "achieves his vision of the angelic world."[30]

The 1980s saw continuing critical and scholarly controversy over the status of *Pym*. John T. Irwin's suggestive theoretical reading in *American Hieroglyphics* (1980) placed the novel in the context of nineteenth-century interest in the Rosetta stone and Egyptian hieroglyphics. He portrayed Pym's voyage as a "symbolic quest for the origin of writing," noting the novel's questioning of its own origins. By placing in doubt Pym's credibility, Poe directs our attention, according to Irwin, to "the limits of knowledge and the limits of written discourse." Irwin further explored the relationship of writing to death, deconstructing Pym's function as narrator as a sacrifice of the living, writing self to the textual, written self. Irwin finally regarded the gigantic white figure as "Pym's unrecognized shadow" and concluded that the narrator's quest for certainty and "primal Oneness" is finally "a death wish."[31] In a 1980 essay Paul Rosenzweig refined and extended the approach of Robert Carringer, elucidating the "enclosure motif" in what he claimed to be "a closely patterned work." He concluded that the profusion of confining images signifies Pym's failure to construct an identity, to constitute himself by absorbing elements of the world beyond himself.[32] In a 1980 article Richard Kopley claimed to have uncovered the "secret" of *Pym* in esoteric associations hinting that the white shape at the South Pole is the figurehead of the *Penguin*, the ship that saves Pym in the opening chapter of the novel. Implicitly challenging the consensus view that Poe completed *Pym* in 1837, Kopley found in the final chapter echoes of a magazine account by J. N. Reynolds published in April 1838.[33]

The signal event of *Pym* criticism in 1981 was the publication of Burton R. Pollin's definitive Twayne edition of the novel. His introduction to the work, his discussion of documentary sources, and his nearly 150 pages of "notes and comments" on the text itself adduced a wealth of scholarly information rife with interpretive implications. Pollin discounted all thematic readings, however—whether "oneiric" or "redemptive"—and insisted that Poe had "low regard for the novel as a finished work of art," though he hazarded the view that *Pym* is a hoax informed by "a mild type of parody" directed at contemporary sea narratives.[34] In an essay accompanying the *Pym* edition, J. V. Ridgely outlined four phases of the novel's composition; he argued that the last sections to be added to the manuscript were the closing editorial note and an interpolated chapter (numbered 23A in the Pollin edition), both linked philologically to Poe's 1837 review of J. L. Stephens's *Incidents of Travel in Egypt, Arabia Petraea, and the Holy Land*.[35]

One year after the appearance of the Pollin edition, Douglas Robinson conducted a comprehensive review of three decades of *Pym* criticism. He called the novel "an interpreter's dream-text" because its eclectic, ambiguous nature lends itself to a wide array of readings. Robinson plausibly divided critical responses into six main types and traced the evolution of different interpretive positions; nevertheless, his survey proved at last to be, as he acknowledged, a "concealed polemic" that privileged the "visionary reading" of *Pym* because—he explained—"visionary critics aspire to a higher level of understanding."[36] In 1982 John Carlos Rowe published a revised and expanded version of his 1977 essay in *Through the Custom-House*; Richard Kopley produced another resourceful essay on possible echoes and allusions, based on the intriguing supposition that Pym's relationship to Augustus projects Poe's guilt about surviving his brother William Henry Leonard Poe, who died (like Augustus) on 1 August.[37]

The visionary reading of *Pym* indeed received fresh emphasis in a succession of studies in the mid-1980s. John Limon's 1983 essay read passages from Poe's 1848 prose poem *Eureka* against episodes in the 1838 novel, finding purported references in *Pym* to concepts of *Naturphilosophie*, or German natural philosophy. He implied, for example, that Poe takes Pym to the polar region to suggest the philosophical movement from the "individualist pole" to the "pole of unity." Ignoring the historical context of South Seas exploration and the cobbled construction of the narrative, Limon argued that Poe's later cosmogony turns *Pym* into a philosophical treatise "retroactively."[38] A more persuasive case for reading the novel in light of *Eureka* emerged in Douglas Robinson's *American Apocalypses* (1985). Because of his teleological emphasis, Robinson focused almost exclusively on the last chapter of *Pym*, which he read as a movement toward primal unity anticipative of the prose poem. But he also regarded the "uncertainty of interpretation" as the "rhetorical focus" of the novel and so construed the ending as Poe's ironic, contradictory effort to signal both the desire for a "transcendental beyond" and the inability of the interpreting consciousness to cross the abyss that separates presence from absence. According to Robinson, the white figure is thus a "mediatory icon," a sign of the desired otherness that both compels and resists analysis, plunging the reader into an "interpretive dilemma" much like Pym's.[39] This sequence of visionary readings culminated in 1987 with another intricate essay by Richard Kopley, which promised to deliver "the *key* to *all* of Poe's *Pym*" by unveiling an elaborate allegory in which the wreck of the *Ariel* signifies the destruction of Jerusalem and in which Pym's deliverance by the *Penguin*—Kopley's theory about the final episode—recalls the dazzling vision of Christ by John of Patmos.[40]

At the same time, new studies focused attention on the novel's self-referential, deconstructive aspects. My chapter on *Pym* in *Poe, Death, and the Life of Writing* (1987) addressed the ongoing problem of interpretation faced by Pym and located the source of the narrator's "hermeneutic perplexity" in his rehearsals for annihilation. Poe represents death as the ultimate unreadable text, an idea dramatized in chapter 10 when Pym reconstructs his horrible misreading of the approaching ship and the "cheerful" tall sailor; the episode demonstrates the "profound indeterminacy" of all texts. Death's blank unreadability, I suggested, also generates the desire to write: Pym's deathlike swoon into a letter-shaped chasm metaphorizes the origin of writing. But, as I concluded, his uncertain survival mirrors the metaphysical anxiety of modernity and casts doubt on the providential design in which Pym wants to believe.[41] In a 1987 essay—reprinted in

Architects of the Abyss (1989)—Dennis Pahl also saw Pym's voyage as "interpretive" and noted how persistently Poe undercuts the narrator's efforts to find meaning. Pahl read the final scene of whiteness not as revelatory brilliance but as "the absence around which the reader is allowed to construct his own interpretive discourse."[42]

In his 1988 essay on the "quincunx" arrangement of the bird nests in chapter 14, John Irwin argued that Poe drew this geometrical configuration—which becomes a model for the mind's relation to the world—from Sir Thomas Browne's essay *Urn Burial* (1658) to show Pym's "ongoing blindness," his inability to see significant patterns around him. According to Irwin, the quincuncial design overlooked by Pym anticipates his failure to recognize the gigantic white form as his own shadow-image. Recasting the argument of his earlier *American Hieroglyphics*, Irwin drew an apt analogy between Pym's perception of the white shape and the perception of each reader: "When one finds one, absolutely certain meaning in a situation where the overdeterminedness of the text makes meaning essentially indeterminate, then the reader is likely not to recognize how much that single meaning is a function of self-projection."[43]

By uncanny coincidence, G. R. Thompson's long 1989 essay (like Irwin's study, first presented at the 1988 *Pym* conference) also hinged on the quincunx pattern as an interpretive key. Thompson, however, associated the configuration with the design of Persian carpets, bolstering his general thesis that *Pym* is an arabesque narrative infused with romantic irony. Subtly modifying the argument of his earlier *Poe's Fiction* (1973), Thompson suggested here that the "framed indeterminacy" of *Pym*—epitomized by the quincuncial imagery—invests the text with an unresolvable tension between meaning and meaninglessness. Despite critical efforts to find order and divine purpose in the novel's elaborate patterning and parallel episodes, he argued, one can never be sure whether this intricacy is "meaningful and necessary, or arbitrary and gratuitous." Seeming to bridge transcendental and deconstructive approaches, Thompson moved back and forth between an insistence on "nothingness" or indeterminacy in *Pym* and an acknowledgment of some impending illumination or truth. He concluded: "The journey's 'end' is to be found in 'the inwardness,' in

God/Self as infinity, paradoxically set 'free' from 'snares of self.'" Yet, maintained Thompson, this last revelation occurs as a rigorously personal, artistic response to the seeming void of the universe itself. So in the end, nothing is—or can be—resolved on the plane of ultimate "meaning." What *Pym* finally represents, for Thompson, is the postmodern dilemma of uncertainty, framed as "textual collapse."[44]

In the present decade, interest in Poe's novel has remained high, as illustrated by the appearance of an important collection of essays (edited by Richard Kopley) and by a handful of provocative studies limning new approaches to the novel. Cynthia Miecznikowski's 1990 article "End(ings) and Mean(ings) in *Pym* and *Eureka*" pursued the familiar strategy of linking the 1838 narrative with the 1848 cosmogonical essay, but she focused on deconstructive strategies and "undecidable meanings" in these texts to argue that the failure of language to convey "ultimate meanings" does not imply an "abyss" of meaninglessness. Rather, it expresses Poe's recognition that "the sublime is beyond the reach of language."[45] Lisa Gitelman's 1992 essay, "*Arthur Gordon Pym* and the Novel Narrative of Edgar Allan Poe," discussed *Pym* as a satirical response to exploration literature of the period. Noting Poe's extensive use of Benjamin Morrell, she viewed documentary passages in *Pym* as deliberate mockeries of the "clumsily self-conscious rhetoric" of *Four Voyages*.[46] Taking a more theoretical approach, David Meakin's 1993 article, "Like Poles Attracting: Magnetism in Poe, Verne, and Gracq," traced the "metatextual" connections between *Pym* and Verne's novel, *Sphinx des glaces*, as well as the complex response to both earlier texts in Julien Gracq's *Rivage des Syrtes*. Meakin emphasized the metaphorical implications of the powerful current or magnetic force that in each narrative suggests a "sheer obsessive desire" for female presence.[47] In a suggestive chapter from *Lost in the Custom House* (1993), Jerome Loving examined *Pym* as "Poe's Voyage from Edgartown"—an American dream that "becomes a nightmare from which there is no ending but only a waking up." In a study concerned with "awakening" as a key trope in American fiction from Irving to Chopin and Dreiser, Loving's treatment of Poe underscored the "alcoholic" pattern of narratives that "take us on a drunk that often ends like a bad dream."[48]

As study of *Pym* moved into the 1990s, however, ideological and political issues in Poe's novel came to the forefront. Returning to the question of race, Dana Nelson delivered one of the most provocative new readings of *Pym* in *The Word in Black and White* (1992). Nelson devoted one chapter mainly to the Tsalal episode, less to indict Poe for his racist portrayal of the islanders than to show how his treatment of Pym and the crew of the *Jane Guy* reveals the exploitative nature of colonialism. By assuming their own cultural superiority and dismissing the natives as "ignorant savages" the white men, according to Nelson, fail to understand the local taboo about whiteness and so fall victim to a fatal plot. She concluded that whatever his own racial biases, Poe somehow grasped the interpretive self-deception in a "colonial knowledge" based on naive, reductive notions of the dark Other.[49] In her chapter "Romance and Race" in *The Columbia History of the American Novel* (1991), Joan Dayan followed a similar approach but explored the issue throughout Poe's writings, focusing on *Pym* for only the last three pages. Dayan suggested that the novel "depends upon a crisis of color," arguing that the allusion to "vengeance" in the pseudobiblical last line of Poe's final editorial note expresses latent guilt and fear of divine retribution for the offense of slavery.[50]

A third recent study pursuing questions of race and racism appeared in *Poe's "Pym": Critical Explorations* (1992), the collection of essays edited by Kopley. John Carlos Rowe's revisionary essay took to task both literary historians who had ignored Poe's complicity in the racist ideology of the South and theorists (including himself) who, in underscoring postmodern issues, had substituted self-referential or metatextual concerns for the "threatening world of material history" from which Poe's fiction always seeks to escape. Rowe insisted that Poe pursued a "racist strategy of literary production" bound up with sexist and elitist pretensions. About *Pym* Rowe contended: "Poe's own repressed fears regarding slave rebellions in the South and the deeper fear that Southern aristocratic life itself might be passing are the psychic *contents* that provoke the poetic narrative." He maintained that Poe's efforts to situate his story in the realm of language and psychosymbolic action betray a need to deny the sociohistorical conditions impinging on the novel, especially the "black savagery" so frightening to Poe's white psyche. Rowe thus suggested that modernist and postmodernist strategies in *Pym* mask the implicit proslavery elements.[51]

Several other essays in Kopley's collection—an outgrowth of the 1988 *Pym* conference—warrant brief mention. A handful of new source studies—by Susan Beegel, J. Lasley Dameron, Joseph J. Moldenhauer, and others—broadened understanding of historic events and extant sources from which Poe possibly drew in shaping *Pym*.[52] Bruce I. Weiner considered the development of Poe's thinking about genre and regarded the several episodes of "deception, delusion, and providential rescue" not as a linear, novelistic scheme but as successive "tales of effect." He concluded: "The writing of *Pym* was not the making of a novelist. It was the means by which Poe mastered and modified the tale of effect and progressed to his major phase as a short story writer."[53] Grace Farrell explored the psychology of mourning in Poe's novel and saw *Pym* as an autobiographical exercise in grieving for maternal loss.[54] Her essay thus resonates with Kenneth Silverman's comments on the novel in his 1991 biography of Poe.[55] Also in the 1992 Kopley collection David Hirsch underscored the dire "postmodern" aspects of *Pym* that prefigure the Holocaust; Alexander Hammond interpreted food, consumption, and cannibalism in *Pym* as tropes of literary production and authorial depletion that allude to Poe's writing a novel for a mass audience; and my own essay considered the scenes of decomposition in *Pym* as clues to Poe's critique of nineteenth-century culture.[56]

Displaying nautical as well as literary insight, novelist John Barth also contributed a witty essay to the Kopley collection. Granting that *Pym* influenced his own novel *Sabbatical*, Barth nevertheless exposed flaws in Poe's "overvalued" work, invoking "the myth of the wandering hero" only to conclude that "the *sense* of the great myth is absent" in *Pym*. He opined that "Poe's novel ought to be regarded as some sort of simulacrum of a novel: not a counterfeit but an isomorph; not a hoax but a mimicry."[57] Ironically, Barth's debunking preceded David Ketterer's fine bibliographical essay summarizing the wealth of critical and theoretical work on *Pym* during the 1980s. Ketterer extended the critical categories used by Robinson in 1982 and predicted "a reconciliation of deconstruction and new historicist approaches" in the 1990s.

Addressing the vexed question of the visionary versus existential or deconstructive reading, he asked: "Why not suppose, reasonably enough, that, in whatever proportion, Poe, with greater or lesser self-awareness, was simply divided between belief in a supernal realm and a corresponding doubt?"[58] Ketterer's overview, along with the other essays in the Kopley collection, testified to the growing regard for Poe's "very silly book."

Despite its novelistic shortcomings *The Narrative of Arthur Gordon Pym* continues to tantalize readers, evoking elaborate interpretations that reveal the condition we share with Pym: the compulsion to explain.

A READING

4

The Preface

Like most introductory documents, the preface to *Pym* was composed *after the fact* to account for the book it physically precedes. Properly read as a postscript, it offers a playful commentary on the already-completed narrative, discussing fact and fiction as inimical concepts, when indeed by novel's end the reported "facts" have become indistinguishable from fantasy. Presenting itself as a clarification, the preface invokes those assumed certainties—fact, truth, veracity—that the narrative itself steadily undermines. The late composition of the preface (which alludes to the end of the novel, set in the Antarctic Ocean) also underscores its troubling relationship to the concluding editorial note. These apocryphal texts, possibly written in tandem, make utterly contradictory claims about the survival of the supposed author, Pym, and the support of his putative literary adviser, "Mr. Poe."

The two installments of the tale attributed to Poe by Thomas White in the *Southern Literary Messenger* in early 1837 compelled the author either to claim *Pym* as his fictional brainchild or to pass it off as a legitimate travel narrative by a native of Nantucket. When the imaginary "A. G. Pym" confesses his authorship in the preface, Poe thereby initiates a scheme of deception; his "*exposé*" (56) is in reality an act of concealment. Dating his testimony "New York, July, 1838," Pym explains how, returning to the United States "a few months ago" (55)—20 at the very least, we may calculate—from an odyssey in the South Seas, he made the acquaintance of Poe, who urged a "full account" of his travels (55). In apparent deference to truth, Pym acknowledges a *"ruse"* that has already occurred: the reticent author has supplied "facts" enabling Poe in the *Messenger* to present *"under the garb of fiction"* (56) portions of his own early experiences. But of course this confession of subterfuge is itself a ploy to explain why Poe's name was thus associated with the periodical excerpts.

Why did Poe want to distance himself from *Pym*? Several stretches of dull prose in the second half of the narrative prompt the suspicion that on the eve of publication the author felt a certain shame about the uneven quality of the work. William Burton, who later hired Poe as his editor, lamented in a September 1838 review in his *Gentleman's Magazine*: "We regret to find Mr. Poe's name in connexion with such a mass of ignorance and effrontery."[1] In writing the novel, Poe had acted against the artistic principles that he later championed: brevity and unity of effect. To satisfy the demands of Harper and Brothers for a "connected story" that would appeal to a popular audience he compromised his standards, spending his talent on an episodic tale derived from earlier chronicles of exploration. Moreover, Poe trotted out every sensational theme in his repertoire, piling on disaster after disaster as if to test the public's appetite for gore. For a writer who entertained lofty notions of his place in the republic of letters, the necessity of writing a rousing potboiler must have entailed humiliation.

But Poe had another reason for wanting to disclaim the narrative. To extract private satisfaction from an onerous project, he devised a hoax to manipulate readers and exploit the naïveté of the American popular audience as he signaled his deeper, ironic purposes to the sophisticated few. The rejection of his earlier *Folio Club* tales as "too learned and mystical" for the masses had hardened his resentment of the reading public, and in *Pym* he tried to get even: he would exploit the public's demand for adventure novels with an exercise in mystification.[2] Perhaps not coincidentally, at about the time he finished the bulk of the narrative (June 1837) Poe published "Mystification," a tale about a clever prankster, Baron Von Jung, who confounds a pedant named Hermann. Von Jung devises a text—a challenge to a duel—in which the language has been "ingeniously framed so as to present to the ear all the outward signs of intelligibility, and even of profundity, while in fact not a shadow of meaning existed."[3] If, as we suspect, this tale comments surreptitiously on Poe's private strategy in writing *Pym*, the preface to the novel likewise casts the unsuspecting American reader as the dupe.

Nowhere is the author's contempt for the public more evident than in the advice supposedly offered to Pym by "Mr. Poe": "He strongly advised me, among others, to prepare at once a full account of what I had seen and undergone, and trust to the shrewdness and common sense of the public—insisting, with great plausibility, that however roughly, as regards mere authorship, my book should be gotten up, its very uncouthness, if there were any, would give it all the better chance of being received as truth" (55–56). Like a confidence man or diddler, Poe praises the "shrewdness and common sense" of his audience as he preys on its gullibility. His low regard for popular taste lurks in the sarcastic suggestion that the "uncouthness" of Pym's style will work to his literary advantage with the general class of readers. Two paragraphs later, Poe directs yet another barb at his audience when Pym reports that although the *Messenger* excerpts appeared as "pretended fiction," alert subscribers refused to accept the narrative "as fable" (56). This reaction reassures Pym that he has "little to fear on the score of popular incredulity" (56): the mass of American readers will believe anything.

Pym's ostensible concern with the difference between fact and fable raises, however, a complicated issue—the problem of representing truth in writing. Noting that for much of his adventure he did not maintain a journal, Pym acknowledges his initial reluctance to take up the pen: "I feared I should not be able to write, from mere memory, a statement so minute and connected as to have the *appearance* of that truth it would really possess" (55). The narrator ingratiates himself with readers by offering what seems a confession of anxiety, a privileged glimpse of the intimate process of writing. This apparent scrupulousness, designed to portray Pym as incapable of falsehood or even of exaggeration, works, however, to legitimize certain dubious assumptions about how truth inscribes itself in a written text. Noting the effect of truthfulness created by writing that is "minute" and "connected" (55) (the latter term perhaps mocking the publisher's demands for a "connected story"), Pym invites us to share the supposition that meticulous detail *implies* careful, informed observation of real things and that copious detail *implies* completeness of disclosure. But these inferences also establish verisimilitude as a mechanism of deception.

Implicitly Poe appeals to the model of descriptive natural science as a method of registering facts about physical phenomena. For Pym a "fact" signifies an unquestionable, self-sufficient truth. Capitalizing on the prestige of scientific discourse, he posits a logical, uncomplicated relationship between language and the real world to which verbal signs supposedly refer. If the language seems precise, then the object it "represents" must surely exist *as such*. Even as this implicit theory seems to validate Pym's later "reports" on the flora and fauna of South Sea islands, his worrying about verbal accuracy glosses over the more fundamental question of the arbitrariness of language and its shifting relationship to the world it purports to describe. His desire to produce an account having the "*appearance* of that truth it would really possess" (55) betrays the radical duplicity of Poe's scheme: while the phrase seems to express Pym's regard for accuracy, it simultaneously manifests an ironic awareness that the "*appearance* of . . . truth" is all that language can ever convey. The preface to *Pym* thus alludes to the unannounced risks we inevitably run as writers and readers because of the slippery relationship between word and world, between writing and truth.

The five treacherous paragraphs of the preface contain another twist: Pym portrays himself as a purveyor of truth, while "Mr. Poe" figures as the periodical fiction maker. By the time we reach the concluding note, of course, these roles will be completely reversed: Poe, "the gentleman whose name is mentioned in the preface" (207), will question Pym's "general accuracy" (207) and confess disbelief about the last part of the narrative. But at the outset, at least, the ostensible author insists on the authenticity of his deposition. He suggests that facts are useful, valuable, and instructive, while fiction is by implication baseless and trivial. His greatest anxiety is that readers will mistake his veridical account for fable; but when Pym professes to worry that his narrative will be received as an "impudent and ingenious fiction" (55), he ironically acknowledges the precise nature of the text, insofar as we can uncover Poe's multiple deceptions. The final paragraph contains perhaps the consummate irony: Poe lies by telling the truth and tells the truth by lying. When Pym insists that in the section supposedly written by Mr. Poe "no fact is misrepresented" (56), Poe paradoxically asserts what is indeed the case—that there are no facts to *be* misrepresented—even as he misleads the reader about the veracity of the narrative in question. Stripped of the rhetorical guise of sincerity, the preface reveals the deeply subversive nature of Poe's private project.

In the closing line of the preface Pym assures even those readers who have missed the serialized episodes in the *Messenger* that it will be unnecessary to indicate where Poe's portion of the narrative ends and where his own commences: "the difference in point of style will be readily perceived" (56). In fact, the stylistic shift is undetectable. In the fourth paragraph of chapter 4, where the periodical excerpts end and the new material (ostensibly written by Pym) begins, the narrative voice is altogether consistent with the one used in the opening chapters. Pym's assurance that the change will be "readily perceived" thus appeals once again to the vanity of readers with shallow praise of their "shrewdness" and discernment. Through various compliments paid to the reading public, Poe carries out two deceitful tasks in the preface— predisposing readers to "put faith in [Pym's] veracity" (55) as he (Poe) insinuates his unmitigated contempt for the fools he must appease. The pseudonymous signature "A. G. Pym" (56)—which may allude anagrammatically either to a "magpie" (chatterer) or an "imp"—leaves a final clue to the mocking ironies that will infuse the narrative to follow.

5

The *Ariel* Escapade

The first chapter of *Pym* begins—as do so many of Poe's tales—in the domain of dull fact: "My father was a respectable trader in sea-stores at Nantucket" (57). Yet the chapter proceeds toward an unbelievable rescue at sea before returning to the realm of the mundane. The opening sequence thus seems to compress the larger action of the narrative, giving us a preview of Pym's voyage—his progressive movement toward the unheard of and the fantastic—and the journey back that finds him (in the preface) conferring with gentlemen in Richmond about his discoveries in the South Seas. The only problem with this interpretation is that Poe drafted the opening episode, the wreck of the *Ariel*, long before he had figured out precisely what would befall Arthur Gordon Pym or how he might be rescued from unspecified calamities to tell his story.[1] But no matter: Poe understood from the outset that popular adventure novels demand a succession of "scrapes" and that first-person, retrospective narration requires the survival of the narrator. A writer could use the manuscript-in-a-bottle ploy only so many times—though Poe in the concluding note seems determined to create a new version of that tactic. The *Ariel* episode (chapter 1) thus served as a model he would use repeatedly in *Pym* to illustrate the narrator's perverse attraction to danger, his impossibly bad judgment, and his largely unconscious talent for escaping destruction.

The narrator's opening declaration, "My name is Arthur Gordon Pym" (57), invites attention to the linked issues of authorship and identity. Numerous critics have noted the patent resemblance to Poe's own name, an autobiographical connection underscored by the subsequent reference to "Edgarton" (57) and less obviously by the details of Pym's schooling and his expectation of an inheritance. But to read *Pym* as a disguised version of Poe's own experiences requires careful discrimination between specific parallels and general or metaphorical connections. Once Pym leaves the mainland behind, it is hard to find precise, plausible analogies to actual autobiographical events. It is harder still to find any justification for reading the novel as a calculated, intricate *roman à clef*, given the urgent circumstances of its composition.[2] Rather, Poe's teasing references in the opening paragraph seem designed to twit readers with veiled allusions to the real Arthur/author, thus establishing his scornful superiority to those unable to discern his implicit signature.[3]

Such deviousness is, of course, consistent with the content of both the *Ariel* episode and the narrative that follows it. First Augustus Barnard goads Pym into sailing at night by claiming to be sober when he is intoxicated; then, after the two lads nearly perish when a whaling ship (the *Penguin*) smashes into the *Ariel*, Pym and Augustus conceal their ghastly misadventure at breakfast the next morning, demonstrating that "schoolboys . . . can accomplish wonders in the way of deception" (64). By representing those events of which the boys' parents remain ignorant, Poe appears to provide the reader with privileged information about what happens during Augustus and Pym's "frolic." But the particulars lack credibility: we are told that Augustus survives prolonged immersion, first in the "bilge water" that fills the *Ariel* and then in the ocean (with a rope wound "tightly" around his neck) after he knocks himself senseless against the bottom of the *Penguin*. Pym's survival is even more miraculous: he reappears "affixed" to the hull of the *Penguin* by a "timber bolt" piercing the sinews of his neck; his body beats "violently" against the plunging ship for several minutes before sailors finally "disengage" him and pull him aboard the whaler

(62). Rather than establishing the narrator's veracity or his willingness to level with his audience, this wild, implausible account raises the suspicion that Pym will deceive anyone—including the reader.[4]

Other aspects of the opening episode likewise prefigure events or images that occur in later chapters. When Henderson, the first mate of the *Penguin*, defies the authority of Captain Block, seizes the helm, and turns the ship around to search for possible survivors of the wrecked *Ariel*, he introduces the motif of revolt that is repeated later in the *Grampus* episode (chapters 4 and 8) and then on the island of Tsalal (chapter 21). The prevalence of this action, usually accompanied by some form of trickery, reinforces the broader interpretive sense of a subversive strategy underlying the entire novel.

Elsewhere, the striking reversals of fortune that cause Pym to vibrate between hope and despair or delight and terror foreshadow the oscillations of the longer voyage on which he soon embarks. These reversals typically hinge on a contradictory relationship between appearance and reality, as when the "mad idea" of Augustus (the proposal to go sailing) seems to Pym "one of the most delightful and most reasonable things in the world" (58). At sea the cool nonchalance of Augustus masks his agitation and mounting terror. The night sea voyage that first seems "mad" and then "reasonable" shortly proves catastrophic and then oddly inconsequential. Deceptive appearances proliferate, but where in *Pym* does "reality" lie? The narrator inhabits a topsy-turvy world in which reason and madness, goodness and evil, fortune and misfortune prove to be unstable, apparently meaningless oppositions. As Edward Davidson reminded us, deception is ubiquitous: "nothing really is what it seems."[5]

Despite its improbabilities, however, the *Ariel* episode poses an apparent contrast between treacherous human reality and enduring spiritual truth. Poe places Pym's misadventure within an explicitly providential context, implying that the hero survives precisely through God's grace and mercy. Significantly, the escapade begins when Augustus swears that he will not go to sleep "for any Arthur Pym in Christendom," a formulation set in contrast to Pym's reply that he is as ready for merriment "as any Augustus Barnard in Nantucket" (58). When the narrator shortly finds himself in desperate straits—Augustus has passed out and Pym (curiously enough) has no idea how to sail his own boat—he tells us: "I recommended myself to God, and made up my mind to bear whatever might happen with all the fortitude in my power" (60). At the exact instant of this supplication the *Penguin* runs over the *Ariel*; Pym feels "the intense agony of terror" (60) and then awakens to find himself saved from death. Explaining how he and his friend have survived, Pym ascribes the rescue to "two of those almost inconceivable pieces of good fortune which are attributed by the wise and pious to the special interference of Providence" (62). Poe could not more blatantly impose a theological perspective on Pym's deliverance. But he then proceeds to have Pym recount the collision and its aftermath in terms that are literally "inconceivable" (61–64). Is Poe asking the "wise and pious" to believe that God saves Pym by impaling him on the bottom of a boat? As we sift through the improbabilities of the rescue, the narrator's patent unreliability as a chronicler of events undermines our faith in his interpretations of God's design, and at the breakfast table, where he flaunts his penchant for duplicity, he gives us even more reason to doubt his providential claims.

Throughout *Pym* Poe repeatedly evokes the doctrine of providence or divine benevolence just when his hero seems doomed to destruction. Although the author admired eighteenth-century works like *Robinson Crusoe* (1719), his ironic treatment of Pym's faith in God (most evident in chapter 10) makes it unclear whether he means to emulate the conventions of the providential novel or to parody them. Do the improbable bouleversements of Poe's plot suggest a meaningful contrast between human chaos and divine order or do they imply that God has disappeared and that Pym's invocations of the deity betray his naive self-delusion? This is a crucial issue for interpreters of *Pym*, and it calls into question the arbitrary assumptions inherent in every act of interpretation. As we see in Poe's self-reflexive novel, Pym's situation often mirrors our own predicament as well— that of imperfect readers of signs, determined to find coherence or meaning or intelligibility in the texts we confront.

Pym fails to recognize the intoxication of Augustus and so fails to discern the risk in the scheme the latter proposes. But does Pym correctly credit his rescue to "the special interference of Providence?" The mere fact of his survival urges such a reading, but if the concept of providence hinges on living rather than on dying, what are we then to make of the subsequent dismal fate of Augustus or of Pym's "late sudden and distressing death" (207) as reported in the final note? If providence implies a higher purpose or destiny, a reason for Pym's "being in existence" (61), is there any evidence that his later violent activities disclose some edifying design?

These questions, of course, point to the long adventure that follows the *Ariel* episode, and they mark an area of basic controversy in *Pym* studies. Readers remain divided as to whether the events leading to the dazzling scene at the South Pole constitute a significant journey toward spirituality, rebirth, and authentic selfhood or, conversely, whether they trace a blind movement toward an abyss of meaninglessness. The contradictory relationship of these positions reflects the essential paradox of the wreck of the *Ariel* and the improbable survival of Pym. By calling the narrator's reliability into question and implying the ubiquity of deception, Poe seems to signal the absence of transcendent truth. But Pym does endure, perhaps through the "interference" of a power that cannot be analyzed or verified but only apprehended through the lens of faith. Appealing to the biblical promise of a heavenly home, Richard Wilbur has contended that *Pym* closes with "the language of homecoming,"[6] an idea that resonates with the three references to "going home" (58–59) that Augustus makes to Pym aboard the *Ariel*. But, of course, the "home" to which the drunken Augustus alludes is the safe, familiar world of Nantucket that Pym renounces in chapter 3 in a remorseless act of duplicity. The disparity between these conflicting interpretations of "home" epitomizes the challenge of *Pym*, a text that seems to defy or subvert all efforts to devise a plausible, coherent reading. Some scholars indeed share the skepticism of novelist John Barth, who insisted that *Pym* has no "thematic center"; it remains for him a piece of hackwork unworthy of critical fetishizing.[7] Many other readers, however, reach a different conclusion, deeming the novel an irresistible, enigmatic text that draws us into its interpretive difficulties through a riveting portrayal of primal passions and through unforgettable scenes of human extremity. For all its pyrotechnics and inconsistencies, *Pym* teases us—like Poe's earlier tale, "MS Found in a Bottle"—with the prospective revelation of some "never-to-be-imparted secret whose attainment is destruction."[8]

6

The Fate of the *Grampus*

If there is a single image in the *Ariel* episode that condenses the symbolic or metaphorical aspect of Pym's experience, it is that of a boat out of control, the *bateau ivre* of adolescent rebellion. Oddly, the narrator does not know how to manage his own craft and with disastrous results entrusts it to the "nautical skill" (59) of his storytelling friend, Augustus. Ironically, when the more massive *Penguin* destroys the *Ariel* and nearly kills Pym, the catastrophe intensifies the narrator's "incipient passion for the sea" (65). He tells us: "I never experienced a more ardent longing for the wild adventures incident to the life of a navigator than within a week after our miraculous deliverance" (65). But without a boat Pym must bide his time (for 20 months), contenting himself with more "stories of the ocean" (65) related by Augustus. Through these tales (half of which are later suspected to be "sheer fabrications" [65]) Pym develops a queer longing for suffering at sea. He entertains visions of "shipwreck and famine; of death or captivity among barbarian hordes; of a lifetime dragged out in sorrow and tears, upon some gray and desolate rock, in an ocean unapproachable and unknown" (65). In this phase of anticipation the boat signifies adventure, freedom, escape from commonplace realty; it becomes a metaphor for the imaginative mind itself.

As Joseph J. Moldenhauer suggested, however, Pym's imagination is inherently perverse. When Pym finally conspires with Augustus in chapter 2 to go to sea aboard the *Grampus*, he hides below decks and promptly consigns himself to the frightening realm of the unconscious. Most readers of *Pym* will grant the aptness of Moldenhauer's further insight that "the ship's hold . . . symbolizes the irrational mind."[1] In the dark, confining space aboard the ship the narrator undergoes living inhumation, confronts impending death, experiences lurid dreams, feels temporally disoriented, receives a terrifying yet unreadable message, negotiates a labyrinth of barrels and crates, struggles with a mad dog, and experiences an agonizing inability to speak. Pym's extended periods of sleep and his concomitant fear of never waking up remind us of the proximity of the unconscious in this literal underworld. As he would later do in "The Fall of the House of Usher" (1839), Poe constructs in the *Grampus* episode of *Pym* (chapters 2–13) an analogical relationship between the containing structure of experience (such as a house or a ship) and the mind of the protagonist thus enabling Poe to give tangible dramatic form to impalpable mental processes. Just as Usher's burial of Madeline in the vault beneath the house represents his effort to repress or seal off tormenting thoughts of his deceased twin, so Pym's enclosure within the hold of the *Grampus* metaphorizes a stage of unconscious obsession rooted in his desire to experience the "suffering and despair" implicit in "the life of a seaman" (65): he becomes the literal captive of all those romantic and patently self-destructive longings that can only be satisfied by a sea voyage. In the course of the novel Pym sails on five different vessels; whether this sequence implies a linear spiritual development (as some critics would argue) or it reflects instead the random unfolding of Pym's existence, Poe's insistence on the ship as an emblem of mind seems crucial to understanding the novel's basic figurality.

Pym frees himself to act out his perverse fantasies through an elaborate strategy designed to deceive his family, especially his mother and grandfather, who oppose his plan to go to sea. To prepare for his escape, he affects a sudden indifference to his nautical ambitions, indulging in an "intense hypocrisy" that pervades "every word and action of [his] life" (66). A letter forged by Augustus, that other teller of fabricated tales, creates the pretext for Pym's leaving home: an invitation, supposedly from Mr. Ross (the father of a friend), to spend the night in New Bedford. But to extricate himself from his past—from the self he has been—this narrator who insists so much on his veracity must carry out one more deception. On the way to the *Grampus* he meets his grandfather and impersonates a "salt water Long Tom," denying his identity and kinship with a rude outburst. This repudiation of the relative whose property Pym had hoped to inherit signals his rejection of material comfort for the sake of that "destiny" he feels "bound to fulfill" (65). It marks the figurative shedding of that home-bound, landlocked self Pym wishes to leave behind.

One of the principal complications of Poe's narrator is that he is simultaneously clever and naive, deceptive and self-deceived. His devious scheme gets him on board the *Grampus* as a stowaway—concealment begetting concealment—but Pym retains an innocence. When Augustus shows him his hiding place, an "ironbound box" said to be "nearly four feet high, and full six long, but very narrow," Pym in his enthusiasm perceives a "little apartment" rather than a potential coffin. Indeed, he compares his pleasure to that of a monarch "entering a new palace" (69), little suspecting that he will soon think of it as his "prison" (78). His anticipation of a cozy literary interlude—Pym escapes from the conditions of his own adventure by reading about the Lewis and Clark expedition—stands in jarring contrast to his later disorientation and panic. When he awakens from a deep sleep to find the leg of mutton from which he had previously eaten now in a "state of absolute putrefaction," (71) Pym experiences "disquietude" but fails to see the rotten meat as a prefiguration of death and decay: he cannot yet perceive this sign *as* a sign.

A subsequent incident displays further misapprehensions. When Pym falls into another stupor his nightmare involves a sequence of threatening scenes, culminating in an attack by a lion; he awakens to find "some huge and real monster" pressing on him. The narrator imagines himself in a "dying condition" and swoons: "My brain swam—I grew deadly sick—my vision failed—even the glaring eyeballs above me grew dim. Making a last strong effort, I at length breathed a faint ejaculation to God, and resigned myself to die" (73). This dire episode, however, turns out to be what Poe (in "The Premature Burial") calls a "bugaboo tale": in a comic metamorphosis, the ferocious "lion" proves to be Pym's slobbering Newfoundland dog, Tiger. Satirically undercutting this staging of impending death and providential deliverance, the scene suggests that Pym's melancholy temperament and perverse imagination make him the victim of his own anxious misreading. He experiences an "overpowering sense of deliverance and reanimation" (73) without recognizing that the only danger from which Tiger has delivered him is his alarming misconception of the situation.

Perhaps the most striking instance of the narrator's incompetence as a reader of signs occurs when he finds a note from Augustus that has been attached to Tiger. Upon discovering that the dog has "devoured" his candles, Pym rubs the note with a few fragments of phosphorus and reports the result: "A clear light diffused itself immediately throughout the whole surface; and had there been any writing upon it, I should not have experienced the least difficulty, I am sure, in reading it. Not a syllable was there, however, nothing but a dreary and unsatisfactory blank; . . . the illumination died away in a few seconds, and my heart died away within me as it went" (78). In his disappointment Pym tears up the note and throws it away, not realizing until later that he has examined only one side of the paper. He accounts for this mental lapse with the excuse that his intellect was "bordering on idiocy" due to bad air, hunger, thirst, fever, and despondency. With more deliberate care, he then locates the three pieces of the note, fits them together, and by a "still discernible glow" determines which side of the paper he has already examined. Applying phosphorus to the reverse side, he sees "several lines of MS in a large hand," but now his own excitement prevents him from reading more than the last seven words: "*blood—your life depends upon lying close*" (80). For someone of Pym's gloomy disposition this "fragmentary warning" conjures up horrible imaginings. To be sure, real danger exists; but this incident serves to point out that in the blackness of the hold, imprisoned in the realm of the irrational, Pym cannot make sense of texts. For him, signs refer not to some extrinsic reality but always to those phantasms that reside in his own chaotic unconscious.

This scene of misreading epitomizes the ongoing crisis of interpretation in the novel. Poe further underscores the issue by subsequently casting doubt on Pym's version of the incident; when Augustus explains how he composed the note, he remarks that the only paper he could find was "the back of a letter—a duplicate of the forged letter from Mr. Ross" (92). If Augustus has indeed scrawled the message in blood on the reverse of the letter concocted to deceive Pym's parents, then logically there should have been writing on both sides of the paper. But Pym assures us emphatically that the side he first inspects is a "dreary and unsatisfactory blank," an empty page (78). Augustus's account contradicts Pym's in a way that places the reader in an unresolvable interpretive bind: was there or was there not a blank side? Did Pym misperceive both sides of the note or has Augustus made up yet another story? Scholars and textual critics have argued that the inconsistency merely illustrates Poe's authorial neglect; they maintain that in writing chapter 5 he simply forgot what he had written in chapter 3, possibly because of a hiatus in the composition. But the meticulous detail in these passages, their relative proximity, and the deliberate pattern of interpretive challenges in the narrative itself—not to mention the fact that the letter in question is itself a fraud—all argue for Poe's "quizzing" the reader with a deception of his own. As John Carlos Rowe pointed out, the paradoxical idea of a page that both does and does not contain writing brilliantly conveys the deconstructive notion of a gap or a space between words and the things to which they refer.[2] Poe was not, of course, a deconstructionist, but his attention to writing and language in *Pym* implies a certain awareness of the slipperiness of words and of the elusiveness of truth as a textual construct.

The subject of the unreadable message, we learn, concerns the mutiny that unfolds on deck while Pym lies dreaming in the hold. By the time Augustus finds an opportunity to slip below and rescue his friend, most of the sailors have been slaughtered. The uprising has stemmed from "a private pique of the chief mate's against Captain

Barnard" (93), who has been set adrift in the Atlantic. Seemingly trivial animosity leads to a revolt and an ensuing scene of "horrible butchery" (86). Pym emerges from the darkness of his womb/tomb into another kind of chaos in which terror and violence have replaced authority and reason. His coming to consciousness—a symbolic rebirth—produces no particular revelation, however, for Pym enters a world as frightening, precarious, and unreadable as the one he has just left. The anarchical impulse that initially prompted the mutiny sets the conspirators (the mate's gang and the cook's gang) against each other in a murderous vendetta. If the ship remains a symbol of the mind, then the bloodshed on board implies the perverse, self-destructive power of irrationality, for the decimation of the crew leads swiftly to the destruction of the *Grampus* itself.

Significantly, Pym leaves the underworld of the ship's hold by assuming the role of a dead man. One of the mutineers, Hartman Rogers, has been poisoned by the mate, and Augustus seizes an opportune moment to tell Dirk Peters, the "ferocious-looking" (87) "half breed Indian" (55) who belongs to the outnumbered cook's gang, about the hitherto unknown presence of his friend. Pym himself then suggests the strategy for overwhelming the mate's gang through his own impersonation of the dead Rogers, the sailor whose corpse (he tells us) was a ghastly sight: "Rogers had died about eleven in the forenoon, in violent convulsions; and the corpse presented in a few minutes after death one of the most horrid and loathsome spectacles I ever remember to have seen. The stomach was swollen immensely, like that of a man who has been drowned and lain under water for many weeks. The hands were in the same condition, while the face was shrunken, shriveled, and of a chalky whiteness, except where relieved by two or three glaring red splotches" (107). Practicing another deception, Pym creates a makeshift disguise by chalking his face, putting on the dead sailor's clothing, and padding himself to simulate the "horrible deformity of the swollen corpse" (108–9). Despite his rational awareness of the hoax, he feels a "violent tremour" at the sight of his own mirror image, for the "terrific reality" (109) of Rogers's decomposition has excited his own powerful anxiety about death.

In fact, when he describes the sailor's death agonies ("about eleven in the forenoon") and rapid putrefaction, Pym recollects a scene he could not possibly have witnessed. Poe indicates that the narrator has remained hidden in his cubicle next to the Augustus's berth until Peters comes below in the afternoon; Pym does not venture on deck—where the corpse has been "floundering" in the larboard scuppers—until evening, when with the aid of Peters and Augustus, he strips off the victim's shirt and drops the body overboard. Although this is his only glimpse of Rogers, whose death he could not have observed, Pym claims to remember those "violent convulsions" and the hideous way the corpse looked "a few minutes after death" (107). Has Poe simply slipped again, writing too quickly to worry about incongruities, or does Pym's "remembering" constitute another "surface game of credibility" about which Walter Bezanson commented?[3] In context, Pym's intense identification with Rogers and his actual handling of the body might explain the discrepancy as a Freudian slip: the "terrific reality" of the corpse has generated in Pym unconscious projections of the death itself. But as an interpretive question, the issue is undecidable; the two versions of Rogers's death cannot be reconciled.

Poe opens the *Grampus* section of *Pym* with a remark that thus gains increasing force: "In no affairs of mere prejudice, pro or con, do we deduce inferences with entire certainty even from the most simple data" (65); that is, interpretation—which always proceeds from assumptions or prejudices—never escapes the condition of its own uncertainty, however confidently it draws "inferences" from apparently simple textual facts. This insight into the difficulty of explication, penned (to be sure) long before Poe had any developed sense of where *Pym* was going, nevertheless seems determinative of much that befalls Pym on his strange journey.

After a successful but bloody countermutiny that relies on the Hartman Rogers ruse, Poe constructs another grim episode that dramatizes the radical uncertainty of interpretation. With the *Grampus* reduced to a half-submerged hulk, the four survivors of the shipboard violence—Pym, Augustus, Peters, and a sailor named Richard Parker—contend with hunger and thirst as they pray that someone will save them: "Throwing ourselves on our knees to God, we implored his aid in the many dangers that beset us; and arose with renewed hope and vigour to think what could yet be done by mortal means toward accomplishing our deliverance" (122). This appeal for more "special interference" by divine providence immediately precedes the appearance on the horizon of "a large hermaphrodite brig, of a Dutch build, and painted black" (123). The ship approaches in an odd, erratic manner, and Pym imagines that he perceives several seamen on board, including a tall sailor "with very dark skin" (123) leaning over the bow and flashing a brilliant smile. As the vessel draws near, Pym and his companions give praise and thanks for their imminent rescue, but Poe undercuts this jubilation in a way that places the notion of providence in a cynical and shocking perspective: "We poured out our whole souls in shouts and thanksgiving to God for the complete, unexpected, and glorious deliverance that was so palpably at hand. Of a sudden, and all at once, there came wafted over the ocean from the strange vessel (which was now close upon us) a smell, a stench, such as the whole world has no name for—no conception of—hellish—utterly suffocating—insufferable, inconceivable" (124). The ship proves to be littered with "twenty-five or thirty human bodies . . . in the last and most loathsome state of putrefaction" (124). As the brig glides by, Pym makes the grotesque discovery that the nodding motion of the tall sailor—which he had earlier construed as a gesture of encouragement—has been produced by a huge sea gull "busily gorging itself with the horrible flesh" (125). Pym's absolute misreading of the situation confirms the impossibility of interpretive certainty; indeed, the chapter closes with his recognition that he will never resolve the "unfathomable mystery" (126) of the ship's fate. But the episode also calls into question the reliability of a providential God and seems to disclose the emptiness of Pym's belief in a divine purpose behind the flux of human events.

This more skeptical reading receives further emphasis when the sea gull rips a "clotted and liver-like substance" from the dead sailor's back, hovers over the *Grampus*, and drops the "horrid morsel" (125) at the feet of Parker. Even as this action suggests to Pym (and presumably to the other men) the unthinkable idea of cannibalism, it also amounts to a death sentence, for Parker (who initiates the proposal) ineluctably loses the lottery and forfeits his life, giving his body and blood (135) to preserve the lives of the others. Does the sea gull signify God's intervention, the operation of fate, or naturalistic happenstance? The answer depends partly on whether we consider the outcome from Parker's viewpoint or Pym's. While from one perspective it seems evident that the gull marks Parker for death, from the other it is far less certain how we should read the dismembering and consumption of the sacrificial victim: is it cannibalism or communion?[4]

As if to justify the revolting developments of the preceding pages, Poe opens chapter 13 with a philosophical reflection on the ultimate interpretation of events:

> Notwithstanding the perilous situation in which we were still placed, ignorant of our position, although certainly at a great distance from land, without more food than would last us for a fortnight even with great care, almost entirely without water, and floating about at the mercy of every wind and wave, on the merest wreck in the world, still the infinitely more terrible distresses and dangers from which we had so lately and so providentially been delivered caused us to regard what we now endured as but little more than an ordinary evil—so strictly comparative is either good or ill. (139)

This perception of survival as providential deliverance expresses either faith or forgetfulness, for the "distresses and dangers" to which Pym refers include the disillusionment of the Dutch brig, the terrible lottery, and the dismemberment and devouring of Parker. Pym's interpretation of past events as divinely ordained thus rationalizes unspeakable happenings, and his conclusion that good and evil are "strictly comparative" (entirely relative) typifies his relaxed theological position. His reckoning betrays an understandable need to construe the horrors that he undergoes as ordered and meaningful rather than random and senseless. For the reader of *Pym*, however, the interpretive issue is different: does Poe appear to validate Pym's providential construction of events or is that view decisively undermined by the narrator's repeated misreadings and misperceptions?

The unexpected turns in chapter 13 do not make this matter any easier to sort out. On 1 August, eight days after Pym discourses on the evidence of God's benevolent care, Augustus succumbs to a gangrenous infection: "About twelve o'clock he expired in strong convulsions, and without having spoken for several hours" (142). Having wounded his arm during the countermutiny, the youth ironically survives the lottery but dies two weeks later—an unexpected development, since Pym had earlier mentioned a conversation with Augustus "many years" (94) after his rescue from the hold of the *Grampus*. We must assume that Poe subsequently found Augustus unnecessary to his plot, and as Daniel Hoffman suggested, the latter's replacement by Dirk Peters as Pym's sidekick may reflect Pym's shift from a rational to a more intuitive mode of understanding.[5]

But what are we to make of the seemingly gratuitous horror of Augustus's rapid decomposition? We know that his arm turns "completely black" (142) on 31 July, but the next day, when Peters attempts to throw the body overboard seven or eight hours after Augustus's death, "it was then loathsome beyond expression, and so far decayed that, as [he] attempted to lift it, an entire leg came off in his grasp" (142). To accentuate the horror, Pym describes the loud clashing teeth of "seven or eight large sharks," which (he asks us to believe) "might have been heard at the distance of a mile" (142). The narrator declines to read the death of his friend as providential; even a decade later, as he composes the account, he can find nothing consoling about it. After impersonating a distended corpse and encountering a boatload of rotting cadavers, Pym must witness the putrefaction of his companion, the youth with whom he has experienced a "partial interchange of character" (65). Interpretation falters here; if Pym cannot draw inferences "with entire certainty" even from "simple data" (65), how can he possibly make sense of the bodily disintegration of his best friend?

Just when we seem to reach the nadir of that "suffering and despair" for which Pym had yearned as an innocent boy on Nantucket, however, Poe gives the story another unexpected turn, signaling this reversal of fortune by the literal overturning of the wrecked *Grampus*.

Pym and Peters have dreaded this predicament, fearing that it would sweep overboard their limited provisions; nevertheless, Pym tells us, "in two important respects, the accident we had so greatly dreaded proved a benefit rather than an injury" (145) by exposing a supply of succulent barnacles and by stabilizing the hulk. The implication seems clear: good may come out of ill, so "strictly comparative" are these apparent contraries. The same principle seems to prevail in the matter of deliverance, for less than a week after the death of Augustus the two survivors sight a ship on the horizon. Although they momentarily worry that the vessel will sail away, leaving them adrift, Pym remarks (with no detectable sense of irony) that "by the mercy of God, we were destined to be most happily deceived" (147). The rescue of Pym and Peters by a British trading schooner, the *Jane Guy*, seems to suggest that God not only works in wondrous ways but also fools us—ever so mercifully—from time to time.

By the time the *Jane Guy* plucks Pym and Peters from their miserable situation, little remains of the *Grampus*, now capsized, disabled, and nearly submerged. In the course of seven weeks Pym's relationship with the ship has changed. We see him first in the hold as a helpless stowaway, next in the cabin as a participant in the countermutiny, then on the listing deck as a victim of shipwreck, and finally on the overturned hulk as a survivor. Though the analogy is not exact—and like all analogies it may be carried to absurdity—Poe seems to imply a rough parallel between the ship's destiny and the fate of the mind. Pym moves from a place of dreams below the decks to the sphere of consciousness and action, but the shipwreck brings on despair and hallucination. Ultimately, its physical overturning prefigures imminent psychospiritual redemption: the arrival of another ship. If the doomed voyage of the *Grampus* defines a phase in Pym's development, it perhaps represents the loss of romantic illusions through an initiation into the deception, violence, and cruelty of human society. But it also reveals Pym's continuing self-deception as a reader of texts and as an interpreter of natural signs; and it reflects his compulsive need to perceive the troubling episodes of his own existence as replete with providential meaning.

7

The Travels of the *Jane Guy*

From the moment Pym and Dirk Peters board the *Jane Guy*, the narrative undergoes a radical change in tone and content, losing much of its dramatic force in the process. This slackening is not without precedent in *Pym*: in the earlier *Grampus* chapters Poe had undermined the dramatic effect of certain scenes with digressions on such nautical topics as "stowage" (97–99) and "lying to" (105–07). Some scholars argue that those earlier interpolations contain sly allusions to recurrent themes in *Pym* or that they comment self-consciously on the process of loading up a text with a ballast of imported material. In chapters 14–17, though, the geographical and historical information dispensed by Pym serves not to punctuate narrative action but to replace it altogether. Perhaps Poe intended to shore up his original illusion of factuality with an infusion of prosaic documentation; as a result, however, his narrator is transformed suddenly from an impressionable, youthful survivor of a harrowing experience into a sober and pedantic man of science engrossed by South Sea exploration. In effect, the chapters sketching the travels of the *Jane Guy* recount a period of sleep and forgetting, as Pym appears to discard the identity that has emerged from the ordeal aboard the *Grampus*.

Virtually the only moment of self-consciousness in this interlude occurs when Pym comments on the kindly treatment he and Peters have received on the *Jane Guy*. Commenting on these new conditions, he delivers a remarkable insight into the psychic effect of radical change or reversal of fortune:

> In about a fortnight, during which time we continued steering to the southwest, with gentle breezes and fine weather, both Peters and myself recovered entirely from the effects of our late privation and dreadful suffering, and we began to remember what had passed rather as a frightful dream from which we had been happily awakened, than as events which had taken place in sober and naked reality. I have since found that this species of partial oblivion is usually brought about by sudden transition, whether from joy to sorrow or from sorrow to joy—the degree of forgetfulness being proportioned to the degree of difference in the exchange. Thus, in my own case, I now feel it impossible to realize the full extent of the misery which I endured during the days spent upon the hulk. The incidents are remembered, but not the feelings which the incidents elicited at the time of their occurrence. I only know that, when they did occur, I *then* thought human nature could sustain nothing more of agony. (148–49)

This remarkable passage sketches a pre-Freudian theory of repression, analyzing the relationship between trauma and memory. Pym concedes that what happened to him on the *Grampus* now seems a "frightful dream" remote from his present circumstances, and he understands that the emotional reality of that experience has been sealed off, consigned to "partial oblivion." But he seems not to consider the implications of this forgetting for his retrospective interpretation of events. Insofar as the *Grampus* section describes a recurrent oscillation between joy and sorrow, it would seem that its primal, traumatic meaning has been buried in Pym's unconscious—hidden from the conscious, rational, providentially delivered self.

Thus released from the horrors of the previous seven weeks and from the gloomy, introspective tendencies thereby exacerbated, Pym devotes himself single-mindedly to the study of geographical, historical, botanical, and zoological data. Poe lards these documentary chapters with paragraph after paragraph of information cribbed—we now know—from dozens of contemporary sources but most heavily from Benjamin Morrell's 1832 *The Narrative of Four Voyages*.[1] Pym's account begins to read like a propagandistic tract encouraging scientific exploration of the South Seas—which in some sense Poe belatedly contrived it to be. Whether there is any literary (that is, novelistic) substance in these chapters is another matter. Several passages have already generated critical discussion: Richard Kopley has associated the narrator's remarks about the royal penguin (151) with the white figure at the end of the novel; Pym's representation of the geometrically arranged penguin and albatross nests on Kerguelen's Island inspired separate lengthy explications by Irwin and Thompson.[2] Certain other details in these chapters invite interpretive conjecture, such as the vanishing islands called the Auroras. By changing Morrell's account slightly, Poe imputes a mystical quality to the uncharted island group: some navigators insist they have seen the Auroras and fixed their coordinates, whereas others sailing in the same latitude and longitude have observed nothing. In this sense, even the details of South Sea exploration display a tension between faith and skepticism. As it happens, the search conducted by Captain Guy yields no evidence of the elusive Auroras: "We were thoroughly satisfied that, whatever islands might have existed in this vicinity at any former period, no vestige of them remained at the present day" (158). For those inclined to read *Pym* as the charting of a metaphysical abyss, this remark has analogical interest.

From the standpoint of narrative structure, the documentary chapters (14 through the first half of 17) serve as a bridge from the *Grampus* episode to the account of the disaster on Tsalal. Poe resolves the problem of getting his narrator to the South Seas from the middle of the Atlantic Ocean by temporarily suspending the journal format begun earlier in Pym's account and providing a summary of the ship's movement while lecturing about islands skirted en route. If this transition has a dull, plodding quality, Poe nevertheless begins to inject into the text more and more hints about the exciting polar destination of his hero. For instance, Pym and Peters learn that, clinging to the wrecked *Grampus*, they drifted an amazing 25 degrees to the south.

This suggestion of an inexorable southward current becomes, by chapter 18, an explicit preoccupation.

Almost certainly Poe had intended from the outset to transport Pym to the South Seas and the Antarctic. In the novel's opening paragraph the narrator remarks that Augustus talked incessantly about his "adventures in the South Pacific Ocean" (57). After Pym's nightmarish stint in the hold of the *Grampus* Poe hints at his geographical terminus more directly when Dirk Peters declares himself "bent upon pursuing the course originally laid out for the brig into the South Pacific." In this key prefiguration Peters tantalizes the cook's gang by discoursing on "the world of novelty and amusement to be found among the innumerable islands of the Pacific, on the perfect security and freedom from all restraint to be enjoyed, but, more particularly, on the deliciousness of the climate, on the abundant means of good living, and on the voluptuous beauty of the women" (93). He later engages Augustus in a "long conversation" about the Pacific Ocean and proposes "a kind of exploring and pleasure voyage in those quarters" (101). As fate (or authorial design) would have it, Pym and Peters are eventually rescued off the coast of Brazil by a ship "bound on a sealing and trading voyage to the South Seas and Pacific" (147). But as anyone with a reliable globe can confirm, the *Jane Guy* never reaches the Pacific, following instead a strange back-and-forth course between the southern portions of the Atlantic and the Indian oceans, tacking erratically southward toward the Antarctic.

The *Jane Guy* thus carries Pym into a theater of scientific discovery, and in chapter 16 the purpose of the ship's voyage undergoes a crucial change. After failing to find any "vestige" of the fabled Auroras, Captain Guy decides that "should the season prove favorable," he will "push on toward the Pole" (158). This move prompts Pym to recite the history of Antarctic exploration from the travels of Captain Cook to the more recent voyages of other captains, James Weddell, Benjamin Morrell, and John Biscoe.[3] In these passages Poe describes ice floes and ice islands as the principal problems of polar exploration, but he also introduces the intriguing phenomenon—reported by Cook, Weddell, and Morrell—of a paradoxical mildness of temperature beyond a certain southern latitude, with an attendant clearing of the polar seas. Such observations, coupled with references to a southern current of increasing velocity, contribute to the mystery that excites Pym's own developing curiosity about this remote region.

Despite his decision to steer toward the South Pole, Captain Guy figures—like Captain Barnard of the *Grampus*—as a hesitant, somewhat inept ship's captain, and his indecision manifests itself in the haphazard course the vessel reportedly follows. Pym concedes that Guy was "a gentleman of great urbanity of manner, and of considerable experience in the southern traffic," but he remarks conversely that the captain seemed "deficient" in energy and that his ship was inadequately armed and equipped, given the "difficulties and dangers of the trade" (147–48). Guy's ambiguous nature reveals itself in his vacillating attitude toward his polar explorations: at the end of chapter 16 Pym finds his own interest piqued by the captain's "resolution of pushing boldly to the southward" (162), but after the ship has sailed further south than any previous vessel, a shortage of fuel and an outbreak of scurvy "impress upon Captain Guy the necessity of returning, and he spoke of it often" (166). At a critical moment, it seems, the captain begins to lose his nerve. Convinced that the *Jane Guy* is approaching land, Pym, on the other hand, finds himself "bursting with indignation at the timid and ill-timed suggestions of our commander" (166) and ostensibly persuades the captain to persevere.

The tensions between Pym and Guy throw into stark relief the dramatic change in the narrator since the start of his voyage seven months earlier. Once a melancholy adolescent racked by fears and deficient in nautical skills, he now portrays himself as an authority on the South Seas, wiser and bolder than a veteran navigator. As the writer of a retrospective account—and thus conscious of the bloody result of his "advice" to Guy—Pym nevertheless congratulates himself on "opening to the eye of science one of the most intensely exciting secrets which has ever engrossed its attention" (166). No longer a boy susceptible to wild dreams, the narrator has become another person altogether: informed, perceptive, and resolute. Pym seems, through some inscrutable process, to have become an adept interpreter of physical signs—or at least this is his delusion as the *Jane Guy* nears the dusky island of Tsalal.

8

The Tsalal Episode

In chapter 17 the narrator infers the approach of land when the crew discovers a huge red-eyed bear on an ice floe; to foreshadow the developing significance of color contrasts Pym emphasizes the "perfectly white" fur of the beast that Peters kills and brings aboard the *Jane Guy* as a "trophy" (165). After a lookout spots "a low rocky islet," the narrator describes a singular ledge "bearing a strong resemblance to corded bales of cotton" (165). This reference—which figures importantly in readings of *Pym* as an allegory of antebellum race relations—indeed evokes an image more reminiscent of Dixie than of the Antarctic. The Caucasian crew finds floating ice, white bears, cotton bales; as several critics have suggested, Poe may be revealing here a secret longing for a racially homogeneous South. But when in chapter 18 the ship reaches a large, wooded island on 19 January (Poe's birthday), the natives who paddle out to the ship break the pattern of ubiquitous whiteness: "They were about the ordinary stature of Europeans, but of a more muscular and brawny frame, their complexion a jet black, with thick and long woolly hair" (168). This scene of cultural and racial encounter forms the principal interest of the Tsalal episode, and Poe's staging of the devious and ultimately fatal relations between the men of the *Jane Guy* and the islanders repeatedly calls Pym's interpretive prowess into question.

Almost as soon as the white sailors make contact with the Tsalalians, the reaction of the latter indicates potential trouble. When Captain Guy hails the approaching canoes by waving a white handkerchief on the blade of an oar, Pym notes that "the strangers made a full stop, and commenced a loud jabbering all at once, intermingled with occasional shouts, in which we could distinguish the words *Anamoo-moo!* and *Lama-Lama!*" (168). Revealingly, Pym designates the natives, the true denizens of the region, as "strangers" in this encounter; he has no sense of being the foreign intruder. Moments later the chief of the natives—whose name, Too-wit, hints at his double-dealing—points to the schooner and utters the very same expressions. Pym notices that the natives "appeared to recoil" from the complexion of the white men (169), but he cannot understand why, as guests aboard the *Jane Guy*, they refuse to approach "several very harmless objects—such as the schooner's sails, an egg, an open book, or a pan of flour" (170). Like the rest of the crew he fails to comprehend the "everlasting *Anamoo-moo!* and *Lama-Lama!*" with which the Tsalalians receive the crew at their village.

Pym's inability to perceive the patterned response to white objects and white skin prevents him from suspecting the deeper meaning of the natives' recoil. His condescending notion of the Tsalians ironically blinds him to the cultural implications of their shared aversions. Thus Pym (who in preceding chapters has represented himself as a prodigy of knowledge) fails to anticipate the ambush that kills the rest of the crew. To the very end of his voyage, the narrator remains oblivious to the taboo of whiteness and thus ignorant of the motives for the massacre. Although he displays his own mistrust of and hatred for the black natives—whom he later regards as "fiendish" barbarians (201)—Pym simply cannot imagine a reciprocal fear and loathing triggered by whiteness.

This cultural blindness manifests itself in several striking ways. Although Pym professes interest in every scientific aspect of Tsalal, calling attention to plants, rocks, birds, and fish, he proves woefully obtuse as an anthropologist. A prime example of this ineptness occurs when he visits the natives' village and observes the entrance of each dwelling site: "At the door of each of these primitive caverns was a small rock, which the tenant carefully placed before the entrance upon leaving his residence, for what purpose I could not ascertain, as the stone itself was never of sufficient size to close up more than a third of the opening" (173). Because Pym comes from a culture in which locked doors keep out thieves, he never considers that the rocks may have a purely symbolic function—as a talisman of protection or sign of absence—in a place where locks are unnecessary. Another source of bafflement is language; revealingly he describes the speech of the natives as "jabbering" (168) rather than intelligible discourse, for what he cannot comprehend in Tsalalian culture he dismisses as nonsense.

What Pym does appear to understand he regards with patronizing amusement. He notes, for example, that the natives seem "afraid of hurting" the *Jane Guy* with their spears, and he plausibly infers that they "believed the *Jane* to be a living creature" (169), but when Too-wit tries to pat and smooth a gash in the deck made by the cook's ax, Pym observes condescendingly: "This was a degree of ignorance for which we were unprepared, and for my part I could not help thinking some of it affected" (169). His Western, rational perspective prevents him and his shipmates from taking seriously the animism of the islanders; thus when the sailors begin cutting down trees on Tsalal, arbitrarily despoiling the island, they pay little attention to the "great astonishment of the savages" (179) and proceed without regard for the local, cultural meaning of their actions. Here Pym's term "savage" tells all: it implies the assumed racial and cultural superiority of the white men, who consider the natives merely ignorant, superstitious folk ripe for commercial exploitation. It further implies the right of the white men to expropriate whatever saleable commodities they may find—a principle Captain Guy attempts to enact by establishing a *biche de mer* industry on the island.

In the tradition of Western colonialism, the men of the *Jane Guy* arrive with beads and bits of colored cloth, expecting to set up a lucrative exchange with "savages" ignorant of the worthlessness of these trinkets. When the islanders welcome the sailors to their village, Captain Guy pledges his "eternal friendship and good will" to Too-wit, proffering "several strings of blue beads and a knife" (175) as equivocal signs of his sincerity. But curiously, the native chief shows contempt for the beads while expressing "unlimited satisfaction" (175) with the knife. In this ceremonial moment, Pym seems oblivious to the hypocrisy of Captain Guy and to the ominous implications of Too-wit's excitement about the knife.

Pym does admit, however, that after the banquet—for the Anglo-Americans, an inedible meal of "palpitating entrails" (175)—the white men connive to discover possible areas of commercial exploitation: "We commenced a series of cross-questioning in every ingenious manner we could devise, with a view of discovering what were the chief productions of the country, and whether any of them might be turned to profit" (176). Although the actual object of this trade is crass exploitation (hence the "ingenious" schemes to pry out valuable information), Pym asks us to believe that the operation is rooted in mutual trust. "Confidence" and "good faith" become the crucial terms in this cynical reciprocity. Exchanging "blue beads, brass trinkets, nails, knives, and pieces of red cloth" for native foodstuffs, the narrator observes: "We established a regular market on shore, just under the guns of the schooner, where our barterings were carried on with every appearance of good faith" (177). But as the allusion to the guns implies, the white men are not trading in good faith, and neither—as we later learn—are the natives: all is "appearance."

Indeed, events reveal that a complex, mutual duplicity exists between the two races. Reflecting after the massacre on the illusion of friendliness created by the natives—who have been thus preparing their fatal trap—Pym manifests a predictable sense of outrage:

> I believe that not one of us had at this time the slightest suspicion of the good faith of the savages . . . and, upon the whole, we should have been the most suspicious of human beings had we entertained a single thought of perfidy on the part of a people who had treated us so well. A very short while sufficed to prove that this apparent kindness of disposition was only the result of a deeply laid plan for our destruction, and that the islanders for whom we entertained such inordinate feelings of esteem were

among the most barbarous, subtle, and bloodthirsty wretches that ever contaminated the face of the globe. (179–80)

In retrospect Pym sees the disparity between the "apparent kindness" of the natives and their actual antipathy for the ship's crew. But he betrays no awareness of the simultaneous deception carried out by the white men to exploit the commercial advantages of the situation. In the same passage Pym claims that, far from feeling suspicious of the natives, the crew entertained "inordinate feelings of esteem" for them. The narrator's own account, however, punctures this one-sided version of "perfidy." On their first visit to the natives' village, Pym tells us, the sailors "took care to be well armed, yet without evincing any distrust" (171). Pym himself nevertheless feels uneasy and communicates his "apprehensions" to Captain Guy; they conclude that their greatest security "lay in evincing a perfect confidence in the good faith of Too-wit" (172). The repetition of the word *evincing* marks precisely the duplicity of the sailors' public demeanor. On the second (and fatal) visit, the crewmen advance on the village "armed to the teeth" with "muskets, pistols, and cutlasses" (180) despite their "feelings of esteem" for the natives. Pym's blindness to the deception of his own cohorts in fact accounts for his inability (despite occasional apprehensions) to perceive the duplicity of the natives. Unconscious of the threat the heavily armed white men pose to the blacks, the narrator cannot grasp the double message in Too-wit's remark *"Mattee non we pa pa si*—meaning that there was no need of arms where all were brothers" (180), an ironic comment on the absence of fraternal trust.

When Sidney Kaplan launched the modern discussion of race in *Pym*, he extracted from the text allusions to the ancient lineage of the Tsalalians that suggest that Poe judged black people to be cursed by God from the beginning of time.[1] But if Poe's account of the atrocity on Tsalal betrays his own racial prejudices and fears—evoking Southern anxiety about another massive uprising of slaves following the Nat Turner Rebellion of 1831—it also produces, as Dana Nelson has argued, a remarkably insightful critique of ethnocentrism and the "colonialist mentality."[2] The recent blanket indictment of Poe as a racist thus overlooks Pym's persistent and fatal miscalculations about the black natives, misreadings generated by his own naive assumptions of ethnic superiority and by his failure as an aspiring scientist to read Tsalalian culture as an intelligible body of distinctive practices and beliefs.

In short, if Pym exhibits colonialist racism he is also portrayed, unmistakably, as a fool who cannot decipher the most obvious signs and portents. In this sense his political consciousness must be distinguished from Poe's. As we see in the concluding note of the novel (208), an anonymous editor calls attention to Pym's almost ludicrous inability to discern the pattern of whiteness in objects repugnant to the natives of Tsalal. His satire of the narrator's self-delusion does not, however, imply a sympathetic exoneration of the natives. Far from idealizing the Tsalalians as "noble savages," Poe underscores the subtle treachery of their scheme to massacre the white men, implying that Pym and his white colleagues have miscalculated the intelligence and resourcefulness of the natives they have tried to exploit with commercial guile. Similarly, he implies that the sailors have failed to comprehend the powerful taboo against whiteness that pervades the island culture. Although the author registers the revolting massacre from an Anglo-American perspective, he compels us to see the event as an inevitable tragedy, given the covert suspicion underlying the semblance of mutual respect. In a sense the conflict emerges from the reciprocal assumption of the other race's malevolence, which becomes for each group a self-fulfilling expectation. Such an interpretation, however, begs the question of colonialism and the subjugation that from the outset it seeks to impose.

From these disturbing—and stunningly modern—questions of racial and cultural difference Poe shifts his narrative back to the more familiar symbolic terrain of the unconscious. By curious coincidence the very cataclysm that annihilates the crew of the *Jane Guy* exposes Pym's old self, the anxious, perverse romantic who has been largely concealed since chapter 14 beneath the persona of the pedantic, empirical observer. Ironically, Pym's yearning for scientific data preserves him from destruction; he steps out of the doomed procession upon noticing "one or two stunted shrubs . . . bearing a species of filbert, which [he] felt some curiosity to examine" (181). Along with Dirk Peters and a sailor named Wilson Allen, Pym enters a crevice just as a "concussion" fills the ravine with rocks, creating the apocalyptic impression that "the day of universal dissolution was at hand" (182). But this is not the apocalypse; although Allen dies in the avalanche—forcing us to wonder why he figures in the scene at all—Peters survives after the narrator extricates him from the rubble.[3] Sealed in a chasm, Pym and Peters yet face a grim situation: they feel "the most intense agony and despair" as they confront the prospect of "being thus entombed alive" (182). This crisis actually marks Pym's second brush with living burial. Having endured confinement in the hold of the *Grampus*, he now finds himself trapped within a rocky fissure—a situation that, even in retrospect, evokes horror for the writer:

> I firmly believe that no incident ever occurring in the course of human events is more adapted to inspire the supremeness of mental and bodily distress than a case like our own, of living inhumation. The blackness of darkness which envelops the victim, the terrific oppression of lungs, the stifling fumes from the damp earth, unite with the ghastly considerations that we are beyond the remotest confines of hope, and that such is the allotted portion of *the dead*, to carry into the human heart a degree of appalling awe and horror not to be tolerated—never to be conceived. (182)

There is an element of comic undercutting here, for the narrator and Peters soon wiggle out of their predicament, finding that "the concussion . . . which had so unexpectedly overwhelmed [them], had also, at the same moment, laid open this path for escape" (184).[4] Rather than attributing the escape to providential "interference," Pym now explains away his good fortune by scientific hypothesis. But this rationalizing fails to hide the fact that the catastrophe has been like a living death. His terrors derive, we see, less from the rock slide than from his own obsessive projection of the fetid conditions of the grave. Like the narrator of the later Poe tale "The Premature Burial" (1844), Pym seems inordinately anxious about a projected interment.

A similar relapse back into his grotesque fantasies of self-destruction occurs in chapter 24, where we see Pym "swoon" as he descends the chasm walls with Peters.[5] Leaning over the abyss, he finds himself preoccupied by the sensations of falling, and he finally succumbs to what Poe in an 1845 tale would call "the imp of the perverse."

> There was a ringing in my ears, and I said, "This is my knell of death!" And now I was consumed with the irrepressible desire of looking below. I could not, I would not, confine my glances to the cliff; and, with a wild, indefinable emotion, half of horror, half of a relieved oppression, I threw my vision far down into the abyss. For one moment my fingers clutched convulsively upon their hold, while, with the movement, the faintest possible idea of escape wandered, like a shadow, through my mind—in the next my whole soul was pervaded by *a longing to fall*; a desire, a yearning, a passion uncontrollable. (198)

Pym sees a "dusky, fiendish, and filmy figure" (198) beneath him and plunges into the waiting arms of Dirk Peters. This passage has generated considerable discussion ever since Leslie Fiedler characterized Peters as Pym's "dark spouse" in a homoerotic reading of the narrative.[6] Whether or not we are willing to understand the relationship in such terms, Pym's fixation with falling involves more than homosexual desire and surely more than weariness and vertigo; his utterance "This is my knell of death!" implies that the scene enacts the antithesis of his premature-burial fantasy—namely, the longing for death. Pym finds himself in the grip of Thanatos; the abyss specifically represents both fear of death ("horror") and release from dread ("relieved oppression"). His uncontrollable longing to fall is the paradoxical symptom of his unbearable anxiety. All the prior episodes in *Pym* that portray the revolting spectacle of decomposition have contributed to the narrator's perverse yearning to die in order to end his agonizing about death.

Of course, the fact that Pym collapses into the arms of Dirk Peters gives the incident a satirical twist and seems to trivialize the anxieties that beset the once-again nervous narrator. By sending Pym down into the chasms of Tsalal, however, Poe recovers some continuity of characterization; the underground experience puts the narrator in touch with his most elemental urges and fears. It also excites Pym's conscious apprehension of "being put to death by the savages, or of dragging out a miserable existence in captivity among them" (185). This gloomy prospect closely recalls his earlier romantic vision of "death or captivity among barbarian hordes; of a lifetime dragged out in sorrow and tears, upon some gray and desolate rock, in an ocean unapproachable and unknown" (65). On Tsalal, Pym's indefinite, adolescent fancies have become real, tangible possibilities.

But what is the symbolic import of Pym's concealment in the chasms? Does his reenactment of chronic fears indicate psychic regression, a retreat from science and rationality toward the primitive and unconscious? Or does it imply the development of a higher awareness that fuses conscious and intuitive understanding? Poe seems to imply the latter when Pym remarks about his fall in the abyss: "On recovery, my trepidation had entirely vanished; I felt a new being" (198). Readers disposed to regard *Pym* as a narrative of rebirth into psychic or spiritual wholeness will find in this remark evidence suggesting the narrator's transformation. But we must weigh Pym's claim of metamorphosis against his continuing penchant for self-delusion and against the flagrant interpretive oversights (summarized in the novel's concluding note) that he makes in the chasms of Tsalal.

Emerging from this network of ravines and caverns, Pym and Peters bring to a close the Tsalal episode by vanquishing a handful of natives, taking a hostage, and paddling away toward the South Pole in a flimsy canoe. Literally and figuratively the narrator seems determined to free himself from the writing in which he is caught; escaping from the hieroglyphic chasms, Pym sets out on what will be his final adventure, his approach to the polar abyss that (as it happens) precisely coincides with his disappearance as a narratorial presence. Poe seems in chapter 25 to concede the hopelessness of Pym's situation and the consequent unlikelihood of stretching out his story more than a few pages. The opening paragraph makes this predicament—which arises from imaginative exhaustion as much as from geographic extremity—explicit: "We now found ourselves in the wide and desolate Antarctic Ocean, in a latitude exceeding 84 degrees, in a frail canoe, and with no provisions but the three turtles. The long Polar winter, too, could not be considered far distant" (201–202). "Regions of ice" (202) prevent Pym and Peters from returning to more temperate latitudes, and their experience on Tsalal discourages them from seeking shelter on one of the islands in sight. Literally and figuratively there is nowhere else to go. The only alternative is the route of paradox, the search for a "still milder climate" (202) at the South Pole.

9

Into the Whiteness

Pym contains several hints in its closing chapters that Poe projected a much longer work. The published version accounts for less than one of the nine years that supposedly elapsed between the narrator's departure from Nantucket in June 1827 and his apparent return to the United States in late 1836. At the beginning of chapter 18, a footnote ostensibly by Pym concedes: "I cannot, in the first portion of what is here written, pretend to strict accuracy in respect to dates, or latitudes and longitudes, having kept no regular journal until after the period of which this first portion treats. In many instances I have relied altogether upon memory" (167n). Regardless of what Poe means by "the first portion" of the narrative—or of how we should interpret this blatant undercutting of his earlier illusion of accuracy—the implication that from 18 January 1828 until the end of his journey Pym was keeping a "regular journal" encourages the mistaken assumption that much of the account still lies ahead. Similarly, Pym alludes at the end of the same chapter to the "vast chain of apparent miracles with which [he] was destined to be at length encircled" (172), thus fostering the expectation that a considerable period of time—the interval implied by "at length"—must elapse before we will see this "vast" array of "apparent miracles" in its entirety.

In another reference to the journal when Pym describes the peculiar shape of the chasms, Poe includes a more explicit prefiguration of episodes to follow. The narrator explains why he has been able to furnish precise drawings of the formations: "I had luckily with me a pocketbook and pencil, which I preserved with great care through a long series of subsequent adventure, and to which I am indebted for memoranda of many subjects which would otherwise have been crowded from my remembrance" (193). Pollin has hypothesized that this remark, like the footnote in chapter 18, was a "later insertion" designed to corroborate the reference in the final editorial note to "two or three" concluding chapters, presumably lost in the "accident" (207) that took Pym's life.[1] But why would Poe insert an allusion to "a long series of subsequent adventure" if he wished to strengthen the impression created in the final note that Pym's narrative is virtually complete? The effect of the comment in chapter 22 is just the reverse. We may infer more plausibly that, at least through chapter 23, Poe himself expected Pym's story to continue well beyond the ordeal on Tsalal, leading to a variety of new situations and subjects.

If it is possible to identify a specific scene that conveys Poe's awareness that he had reached a narrative impasse, it may well be the moment in chapter 24 when Pym emerges from the chasm in a location reminiscent of "those dreary regions marking the site of degraded Babylon." Surrounded by "huge tumuli," ancient burial stones, Pym imagines these to be the ruins of "some gigantic structures of art," but he concedes in the same breath that "in detail, no semblance of art could be detected" (198). Extricating himself from chasms that resemble "alphabetical characters" (195), Pym confronts a contradictory sort of wreckage that seems at once artful and artless. We may surmise that here Poe metaphorically surveys the shambles of his own unfinished narrative; his insistence that "no semblance of art could be detected" may be a derisive, self-conscious reference to the novel he could already see falling to pieces. The appearance of this ambiguous image so close to chapter 25—which acknowledges Pym's terminal situation—strengthens our suspicion that here Poe perceives the collapse of his own narrative structure.

Whether the final chapter presents an abortive ending or a "complete and fully executed" conclusion has more than casual significance for the interpreter of *Pym*.[2] Since readings that construe the final scene as a transfiguration, a deliverance, or a rebirth presume a high degree of intentionality and cohesiveness in the elaboration of Pym's fate, the problem hinges on the question of expediency. As we know, Poe composed chapter 25 to give his incomplete—and perhaps unfinishable—narrative a semblance of closure. But did he craft the last episode to emphasize the spiritual or mythic aspect of Pym's journey—thus underscoring the serious content beneath its gruesome and deceptive surface—or to turn the story into a deliberate mystification, thereby manifesting his scorn for the reading public and his frustration with the generic demands of the novel? To put the question another way, does the last dazzling vision confirm a theological design—a providential scheme that has been implicit all along—or does it amount instead to narrative razzle-dazzle, a way of masking the abrupt and arbitrary suspension of a story that had become for Poe quite literally interminable? Does the conclusion in fact flout the novelistic convention of providential deliverance, thus revealing Poe's own cynicism about divine intervention?

These questions cannot easily be resolved, for Poe's final chapter hints at his fundamental ambivalence. On the one hand, Pym remains in a state of self-delusion, betraying his inability to comprehend either the taboo of whiteness or the reason for the massacre of the white men. He cannot understand why his hostage, Nu-Nu, reacts so fearfully to the sight of (presumably white) linen shirts rigged as makeshift sails for the canoe. When he questions the native about the "motives of his countrymen" for killing the crew, he cannot comprehend Nu-Nu's response—revealing his black teeth—and dismisses his "idiotic gesticulations" (205). Yet Poe clearly expects the attentive reader to perceive this clue to the basic black-white conflict so pivotal to the whole Tsalal episode. This sustained stupidity on the narrator's part undermines the notion that his passage into the polar whiteness possesses deep spiritual import, and in so doing puts the last portion of his story in an ironic perspective.

Despite Pym's shortcomings, we must as readers nevertheless acknowledge the rhetorical force and haunting imagery of the narrative's final pages. Slipping back into the journal format he last used in chapter 18, the narrator signals the onset of an extraordinary experience when he remarks on 1 March that "many unusual phenomena now indicated that we were entering upon a region of novelty and wonder" (203).[3] Pym describes a gray vapor on the horizon, "flaring up occasionally in lofty streaks" (203), and notes inexplicable changes in the temperature and color of the ocean. As the days pass, the increasingly warm water becomes milkier in its "consistency and hue." The "wild flickerings" on the horizon coincide with great perturbations of the polar sea; a "powerful current" seizes the canoe and Pym feels himself overcome by "a *numbness* of body and mind—a dreaminess of sensation" (204). The strange torpor persists, the water becomes unbearably hot, white flakes of an ashy material begin to fall, and on 9 March, Pym likens the distant vapor to the spray of some "limitless cataract, rolling silently into the sea from some immense and far-distant rampart of heaven" (205). Emphasizing the relentless current, Poe seems to represent the hypothesis—popularized in the 1820s by John Cleves Symmes—of a vortex at the South Pole drawing into itself all the waters of the earth.[4]

After an interval of 12 days (for which the narrator makes no effort to account), the canoe approaches the gigantic curtain of vapor at "a hideous velocity," and on 22 March, Pym and his companions face the abyss: "And now we rushed into the embraces of the cataract, where a chasm threw itself open to receive us. But there arose in our pathway a shrouded human figure, very far larger in its proportions than any dweller among men. And the hue of the skin of the figure was of the perfect whiteness of the snow" (206). These sonorous lines and the images of the cataract, chasm, and "shrouded human figure"—which have provoked more critical disagreement than any other brief passage in Poe's writings—leave Pym suspended forever on the verge of a "never-to-be-imparted secret whose attainment is destruction."[5] Together with the discovery that Nu-Nu's spirit has "departed," the reference in this entry to "pallidly white birds" flying from "beyond the veil" supports the notion that this "region of novelty and wonder" (203) is precisely the realm of death. Geography has given way to metaphysics: what looms before Pym is not the South Pole but a gigantic figure of perfect whiteness, an image—as some critics have insisted—of divine presence at the threshold of the eternal. On the brink of apparent annihilation, the narrator confronts what may be a definitive embodiment of that "special interference" (62) that has delivered him repeatedly throughout the narrative from destruction—or so we might infer from the resonant, biblical heft of the last lines, which convey the idea of a sacred moment. Indeed, the absolute purity of the shrouded figure recalls the radiance of many Old and New Testament manifestations of holiness.

Critical speculation about the meaning of this figure—and thus the nature of Pym's fate—reflects a wide range of interpretive possibilities, of which we may discern three main arguments. The first is naturalistic, often based on the travel accounts of writers like Jeremiah Reynolds or William Scoresby, which associate the white form with plausible physical phenomena (polar bears, penguins, icebergs). By locating precedents for Pym's observations in earlier exploration narratives, such interpretations imply that, to the very end, Poe worked to maintain verisimilitude and to depict credible natural phenomena. The second line of critical speculation comprises the mythic, supernatural, or spiritual readings that identify the figure as an image of the reborn self, as an angelic presence, as Christ, or even as God, the "Ancient of Days." In this interpretive scheme, symbolic significance attaches to the fact that Pym's voyage occupies exactly nine months—the term of human gestation—signifying a type of rebirth.

Finally, the third approach encompasses the skeptical or deconstructive interpretations that construe the giant "human" form as the narrator's delusion or as an optical illusion—hence an authorial deception and a false ending—since, as it happens, Pym has not gone to meet his Maker nor has he plunged to an underwater death.[6] Instead, as the final note informs us, he has somehow made his way back to the United States, where after meeting his actual literary creator—Mr. Poe of Richmond—he has "perished" in a commonplace "accident" (207) after delivering most of his narrative to the publisher. The abrupt and arbitrary manner in which Poe dispatches Pym recalls his similarly cavalier elimination of Augustus and calls into question the mysticism of the final scene.

After four decades of critical discussion, we may observe that most interpretations of the novel's ending have seemed unsatisfactory because they attempt to ignore or rationalize part of its inherent ambiguity. Douglas Robinson in *American Apocalypses* examined conflicting implications more judiciously than any previous analysis but finally privileged the spiritual or transcendental perspective.[7] Readers inclined to accept Robinson's conclusions may find my own effort to articulate *Pym's* contradictions skewed in the direction of deconstructive irony. Several commentators have recently remarked that the only certainty about the novel's ending is its function as a test of critical will: its very opacity invites and demands exegesis even as it defies adequate explanation. What the darksome glare of the polar sky perhaps ultimately reflects is the reader's own interpretive predisposition. Insofar as the meaning of Pym's adventure culminates in this scene, the narrative at last proves inscrutable. Like the German text mentioned in Poe's "The Man of the Crowd" (1839), *Pym* resists coherent interpretation: "*Er lässt sich nicht lesen*" (it does not permit itself to be read).

In a peculiar way the last chapter thus reveals the extent to which our predicament as interpreters of *Pym* mirrors the ongoing dilemma of the narrator himself. At every juncture, Pym tries to impose his own interpretive grid on the chaotic, shifting conditions of phenomenal experience. But Poe repeatedly dramatizes the failure of this hermeneutic project by exposing the misperception and self-delusion to which Pym is prone. The narrative thus comprises a protracted adventure in misreading. Yet as Pym's questions to Nu-Nu in chapter 25 indicate, the urge to achieve a coherent understanding of events persists. In this way, Poe's novel delivers an ironic critique of our human compulsion to *make* sense, literally to manufacture meaning; intelligence abhors a cognitive vacuum and must fill a discernible void with signification.

This primal gesture of explication before the abyss of interpretive anxiety, so much a part of Pym's experience, ultimately mirrors our own radical fear of uncertainty and ambiguity. It allows us to see the limits of our own knowing as an unspoken source of apprehension and suggests that we generate interpretation in some sense as a defensive reaction to the overwhelming unknowableness of so much that defines our mortal condition. As Poe suspected, what terrifies us most is the anomalous and the unnameable, that which cannot be reduced to linguistic formulation or empirical explanation. Curiously enough, Pym makes no effort to speculate about the nature of the "shrouded human figure" rising up before the polar chasm, but his predicament continues to arouse interpretive anxiety in critics who feel compelled either to account for this shape—with greater or lesser displays of ingenuity—or to dismiss it (as Henry James did) as an impertinence. In reality, though, the image can be neither explained nor avoided. Resisting attempts to rationalize its function, it continues to generate interpretations that corroborate each reader's assumptions about Poe's intentions. In a sense, the varying responses to the white form reflect the implicit circularity of most criticism—in which conclusions reiterate initial suppositions—and enable us to glimpse the urgent self-reassurance that informs human efforts to make sense or to construct meaning in the face of the abyss.

Poe's strategy of breaking off his narrative at a climactic moment and leaving unresolved the identity of the looming figure seems calculated to produce the sort of mystification he loved to produce in the popular audience. But it also brings us back to the text of *Pym* and to the problem of the taboo attached to whiteness. As the canoe nears the polar chasm, the narrator observes floating in the water "one of the white animals whose appearance upon the beach at Tsalal had occasioned so wild a commotion among the savages" (205). His remark alludes to the bizarre scene at the end of chapter 22 in which the explosion of the *Jane Guy* propels ashore the body of a small, short-legged animal with "scarlet teeth and claws," which the crew had earlier picked up at sea on 18 January. The natives react to the appearance of the carcass by keeping a careful distance from it, surrounding it with stakes, and screaming *"Tekeli-li!"*—the very cry that accompanied the destruction of the ship beforehand (190–91). This passage connects importantly with Pym's final journal entry of 22

March, for he notes of the gigantic birds that fly from the far side of the white veil that "their scream was the eternal *Tekeli-li!*" (206).

Whether his intent is to deceive or stupefy the reading public, here Poe seems determined to connect the Tsalalian taboo with the scene of pure whiteness at the South Pole. Freud reminds us that the concept of taboo is itself paradoxical, leading in two opposite directions: it implies both the sacred, or consecrated, and the unclean, dangerous, or forbidden.[8] In a rational scheme of values, this doubleness makes little sense, for how can something be holy and horrible at the same time? Yet in the logic of the unconscious that Freud elucidates, this split refers to an inherent ambivalence in the root concept of the untouchable, unspeakable, and uncontrollable; that is, the idea of the taboo acknowledges the fearful power of that which cannot be contained and regulated, that which cannot be demystified by interpretation. The white figure marks the limit of human knowing and the threshold of the numinous; thus it remains inexplicable, irreducible, and—to modern critics of *Pym*—relentlessly disconcerting.

10

The Concluding Note and the
Problem of Meaning

We will never know the precise circumstances that caused Poe to halt his narrative in such an inconclusive way. For pragmatic reasons, he may have decided—as he did later in the tale "The Mystery of Marie Rogêt" (1842)—to leave the final enigma unresolved to avoid the embarrassment of having his own version of the "truth" contradicted by an unfolding contemporary investigation, in this case "the governmental expedition [then] preparing for the Southern Ocean" (207). Perhaps under the pressure of time and with a growing sense of the unwieldiness of the novel, he capitulated to imaginative exhaustion and summarily finished off his hero. Or perhaps he saw his unfinished cliffhanger as a kind of intellectual revenge against a reading public whose "shrewdness and common sense" he covertly ridiculed (55). In the late spring of 1837, as Poe composed the preface, the concluding note, and the "hieroglyphic" chapter 23—roughly at about the time he drafted his review of J. L. Stephens's *Incidents of Travel in Egypt, Arabia Petraea, and the Holy Land*—he must have felt considerable pressure to finish the book so as to capitalize on the growing excitement about South Sea exploration. Contrary to popular expectations, however, the Wilkes Expedition did not sail to the region until August 1838, and (as Alexander Hammond has speculated) Harper and Brothers apparently shelved Poe's manuscript for commercial reasons, waiting until the imminent departure of the fleet to put the book into print near the end of July.[1]

Whatever his motives, Poe's addition of the final editorial note radically alters the effect of *Pym*, producing (among other results) a sense of anticlimax with the disclosure that although the narrator has somehow survived his adventure near the South Pole, the final chapters recounting his escape from death have been lost, ironically, in the local "accident" that has claimed his life. To accomplish this mystification, Poe speaks of the circumstances surrounding Pym's "distressing death" as a matter "well known to the public through the medium of the daily press" (207). He thus compels contemporary readers either to accept the fabrication at face value or to feel grossly uninformed. Beyond his stunning announcement, so contrary to the expectations raised by a preface dated July 1838, and signed by a still-living narrator, the note injects many unsettling revelations and remarks that collectively put in doubt not only Pym's fate but also his reliability as a narrator, the presumed authority of his interpretive comments, and even the belief of "Mr. Poe" in Pym's veracity. If we regard the note as an integral part of the narrative, such undercutting forces us to rethink the entire text and subverts those readings that ascribe to *Pym* a philosophical or theological seriousness.[2]

This brief text actually serves a variety of rhetorical purposes. In the first paragraph, as several scholars have remarked, Poe seems determined to prepare the way for a second narrative, should his novel meet with commercial success.[3] Although the unnamed author of the note fears that the narrator's last chapter has been "irrecoverably lost," he adds: "This, however, may prove not to be the case, and the papers, if ultimately found, will be given to the public" (207). Another strategy for a companion volume emerges in the second paragraph, when the writer observes that "some information might be expected" from Dirk Peters, who has also survived the polar adventure. Although Peters has not yet been contacted by the publisher, "he may hereafter be found, and will, no doubt, afford material for a conclusion of Mr. Pym's

account" (207). Poe thus positioned himself to dash off a sequel if
Pym—contrary to expectations—enjoyed a modicum of popularity.

But the author's basic pessimism about the book's prospects
apparently prompted his ironic scheme of distancing himself from the
narrative by announcing the refusal of "the gentleman whose name is
mentioned in the preface" (Poe himself) to "fill the vacuum" by sup-
plying those missing chapters himself. The anonymous editor reports
that Poe has declined because of "the general inaccuracy of the details
afforded him"—presumably by Pym—and (more disturbingly) because
of his "disbelief in the entire truth of the latter portions of the narration" (207). Since Poe figures in the preface as Pym's sponsor and col-
laborator, this eleventh-hour disclaimer implies a rift between the
former associates and raises new questions about Pym's believability.
By implication, "Mr. Poe" withdraws his previous endorsement of
Pym's veracity and casts doubt on the part of the account that concerns the polar region. Although we never learn which specific elements of the narration have aroused Poe's suspicion, such information
is beside the point. By professing his disbelief, Poe undermines the illusion of credibility established in the preface, creates uncertainty about
the status of the text, and in effect disavows his collaborative role in
the project. Whether motivated by anticipatory shame or by a puckish
desire to confound unsuspecting readers, Poe's renunciation produces
an immediate interpretive problem for all readers by imputing to
Arthur Gordon Pym—whose spiritual transformation has preoccupied
so many critics—a devious unreliability.

Ironically, the anonymous editor who has reported the disillusionment of Mr. Poe seems to defend Pym by declaring that it would
give him "much pleasure" to "throw credit" on the "very singular
pages now published" (207). But his effort to validate the narrative by
commenting on the chasms of Tsalal has the converse effect of making
explicit Pym's interpretive lapses and limitations. Noting the narrator's
refusal to see the "indentures" as ancient inscriptions, the editor
remarks that even Mr. Poe has overlooked their "alphabetical" nature,
and he proceeds pedantically to lay out "the facts in relation to *all* the
figures." His consequent reading of the chasms themselves as formations resembling the Ethiopian word for 'to be shady' initiates a com-

plex philological exercise that uncovers writing within writing: on the walls of the crevasse are Arabic and Egyptian hieroglyphs that connect the idea of whiteness to the phrase "the region of the south." Coupled with Nu-Nu's disclosure in chapter 25 that the king of the remote southern islands is named "*Tsalemon* or *Psalemoun*" (203), this philological information raises the suspicion (as many commentators have pointed out) that the natives may indeed be descendants of the Israelites—specifically, the cursed sons of Ham.[4]

Important as this connection may be for the racial allegory embedded in the Tsalal episode, it exposes in a new, direct way Pym's failure as a reader of signs. His stubborn refusal to see the inscriptions *as writing*, as intelligible signs, blinds him to any message they might convey. Thus he misses the coded implication—the southward reach— of the crude hieroglyph that resembles "a human figure standing erect, with outstretched arm" (195), and he even undertakes to persuade Dirk Peters of the "error" of assuming human meaning. In the final note, however, the editor exposes Pym's blunder, calls attention to the patently pornographic caricature, and informs us that his own linguistic studies have provided "strong confirmation of Peters's idea" (208). Moreover, in the final paragraph this unnamed exegete traces the pattern of whiteness and notes the aversion of the natives, thereby explicating the taboo that has escaped the narrator's comprehension. As he labors to "throw credit" on Pym's account, the editor ironically reveals Pym's colossal obtuseness, placing in doubt not only the narrator's adherence to "fact" and "truth" but also the credibility of those interpretive gestures that pervade his narrative.

This successive discrediting—Mr. Poe challenges Pym's veracity, the editor exposes both Pym's mistakes and Poe's oversight—compels us to ask why, in the last analysis, we ought to accept the editor's construction of "truth" as decisive and definitive. The unraveling of Pym's interpretation finally suggests that all representations of meaning— even the possibility of meaning itself—may be denied or discredited by a later commentator operating with different assumptions or focusing on contradictory information. If *Pym* enables us to "know" anything, it is the arbitrary, improvisational nature of interpretation, which creates the effect of knowledge or insight largely by suppressing contrary

evidence or interpretive uncertainty and by asserting an authority rooted in its own posterior status as (literally) the latest word on the subject. The editor of the concluding note attempts to have literally the
last word in *Pym* by correcting both Poe and Pym as he places the narrative in a new, problematic light. His critique implies that if the putative narrator as well as the former editor of the *Southern Literary
Messenger* have misconstrued key details about Tsalal, other "errors"
may pervade their collaborative text.

But this progressive undermining of interpretive authority calls
into question the reliability of the editor himself, pushing us toward a
skeptical reexamination of the text's actual last words. At the end of
the note stands a strange, italicized sentence within quotation marks:
"*'I have graven it within the hills, and my vengeance upon the dust
within the rock'*" (208). No explanation accompanies the line, which
has an Old Testament resonance. But just who is being quoted, and
why is the sentence in italics? In a scholarly gloss to the text, Pollin
assumed that the italicized citation is "clearly an indication that Deity
is speaking" (362n). His gloss ignores the problem, however, of who is
writing—who purports to mediate, in this instance, between God and
the reading public. Although the line bears some resemblance (as
Pollin notes) to Job 19:24, it does not in fact derive from the Bible.
Should we assume that the supposed editor has been inspired by God
to insert the line as a divine sanction of *his* interpretation of the writing "graven . . . within the hills" of Tsalal? Such an inference might
support the view (developed by Kaplan) that God has cursed the
Tsalalians for eternity and has inscribed His doom on the rocks in
three ancient languages.[5] Or is this pseudobiblical postscript the work
of an anonymous hand capping the editor's commentary with a cryptic utterance that challenges *his* authority? An interpretation along
these lines would be consistent with the overall dismantling of authority inherent in the note and would imply that not even the pedantic
editor has grasped the revenge of the natives as a prefiguration. Rather
than reinscribing the curse on the sons of Ham, the sentence perhaps
alludes (as Joan Dayan suggested) to the "offense of slavery" and thus
to some "inevitable catastrophe" or sacred vengeance to be visited
upon the South.[6]

Alternatively, the declaration may be Poe's own scandalous appropriation of the Creator's voice to reassert his authority over the text. John Irwin remarked that the sentence operates as "an encrypted signature—the author's signature for the whole work," referring (as did Maurice Mourier) to the "graven" message in the chasms (207) that forms the initials *E.A.P.* At the same time, Irwin contended, the allusions to "dust" and engraving also pertain to the grave and to the problem of death, the silence that marks the dead end of language (as it were), the "unbreakable crypt" that cannot be deciphered. If language comprises a system of signs referring to the phenomenal world, the word *death* figures inevitably as an empty signifier pointing to a gap or an abyss that cannot be bridged linguistically. Irwin thus plausibly concluded that the author's claim of "vengeance" refers to "the revenge of art" against "time, change, and mortality, against the things that threaten to obliterate all trace of his existence."[7] In this sense *Pym* and the corpus to which it belongs constitute Poe's literary defiance of death.

To think of *Pym* as a monument, however, is to recall those ruined "gigantic structures of art" (198) in chapter 24 that appear to metaphorize the collapse of the narrative and to imply Poe's despairing view of the project. If we consequently understand the note as a last exercise in mystification and mockery, we may interpret the closing reference to the chasmal *E.A.P.* and to its "Ethiopian" (207) etymology either as an allusion to the "shadow or darkness" that has become the real author's trademark or (more radically) as a sly acknowledgment of the "shady," or dishonest, nature of the novel itself.[8] The latter reading accords with the supposition that Poe regarded his self-canceling hoax as an act of retribution against the popular audience and its appetite for literary "uncouthness" (55–56). In this sense the apparently biblical malediction may be said to express the author's private contempt for those readers deceived by his ploy.

In a broader sense, however, the contradictory implications of the final line take us back to the ambiguity of the work as a whole. E. D. Hirsch commented that an interpreter's preliminary assumptions about the genre of a text are constitutive of everything he or she subsequently infers; that is, our initial surmise about literary type carries a whole set of expectations about the nature and content of embedded meanings.[9] To be sure, some works provide clearer generic signals than others and thereby restrict the range of reasonable interpretation. In the case of *Pym*, however, different readers continue to make fundamentally different suppositions about its controlling form. The textual reality is that there is no stable generic principle; Poe vacillates between fact and fantasy, between symbolism and satire, between parable and parody, working out the deeply conflicted motives of his narrative scheme.

As we confront the difficulties of interpreting *Pym*, its errors, incongruities, and banalities also demand attention and collectively sound a cautionary note against "overingenuity" in our construction (or deconstruction) of meaning.[10] There is a distinct possibility that Poe had the novel in mind when in July 1838 he begged Secretary of the Navy James Kirke Paulding for a clerical position with the U.S. Navy: "Could I obtain the most unimportant clerkship in your gift—*anything, by sea or land*—to relieve me from the miserable life of literary drudgery to which I, now, with a breaking heart, submit, and for which neither my temper nor my abilities have fitted me, I would never again repine at any dispensation of God."[11] The "literary drudgery" inimical to his "temper" and "abilities" may well refer to some recent task—perhaps proofreading—associated with the final preparation of *Pym* for publication. In any event, Poe (typically given to editorial self-congratulation) made no boast about his novel and in his only surviving comment about it—a 1840 letter to William Burton—dismissed its importance.

Despite its inconsistencies and improbabilities, however, *Pym* remains a provocative, unforgettable narrative. In a tale of adventure that seems anything but philosophical, the numerous episodes that hinge on the hero's efforts to interpret overwhelming phenomena foreground the issues of knowledge, meaning, truth, and divine providence. The question of providence becomes singularly vexed, for Pym routinely calls attention to the providential aspects of his nightmarish experience. In the opening chapter in which the *Penguin* smashes into Pym and Augustus aboard the *Ariel*, the narrator explains that their survival has been effected by some "almost inconceivable bits of good

fortune which are attributed by the wise and pious to the special interference of Providence" (62). Pym subsequently invokes the idea of
divine protection at the end of chapter 13, where he notes that "by the
mercy of God" he has been saved from death by the appearance of the
Jane Guy (147).

Yet as noted earlier, Poe complicates the providential theme in
chapter 10 by inserting it unmistakably into Pym's account of the ship
of death. Seeing the Dutch brig approach "more steadily than before,"
Pym and his cohorts construe this change as a sign of benevolent purpose, but in the very act of thanking God "for the complete, unexpected, and glorious deliverance" immediately at hand, they are overcome
by "a smell, a stench, such as the world has no name for" (124). This
juxtaposition of "glorious deliverance" with an unbearable stench not
only shatters Pym's assumptions about the ship and its crew but also
calls into question his presumption of a providential scheme under-
writing his survival.

The problem of destiny undergoes further complication, for
throughout *Pym* (at the beginning of chapter 13, for example) Poe
contrasts passing allusions to providential deliverance with constant
references to fate and fortune. He thus evokes a philosophical controversy stretching back by way of Milton to Boethius. By a stroke of
"good fortune" Pym conceives the idea of impersonating a dead sailor
during the struggle for control of the *Grampus* (107); by "great good
fortune" he manages to reach the floating hulk of the vessel that has
keeled over in rough seas (144). Providence and fortune actually des-
ignate conflicting notions of futurity—one grounded in faith in a car-
ing God who orders events and intervenes in personal lives to assure a
certain outcome, the other in a pagan concept of *fortuna,* or blind
luck; one presumes the efficacy of divine will in the unfolding of history, the other supposes the operation of random chance. In other
words, belief in providence assumes the existence of a coherent plan
behind the uncertainties of experience, while trust in fortune implies a
resignation to the absurd unpredictability of events—metaphorized by
the spinning of a wheel—and to the absence of a controlling design.
From this perspective we may note that Pym's earliest invocation of
providence in chapter 1 hints at his confusion: his rescue from the

Ariel occurs, he remarks, *either* through "good fortune" or through the "special interference" (62) of a providential power.

This philosophical split at the heart of the narrative deeply complicates our understanding of the final chapter, for the suspension of Pym's narrative may represent either completion of his spiritual quest or—more skeptically—his arbitrary erasure as a narrator. Whatever the distractions besetting Poe as he composed *Pym*, his story brings us back insistently to the problem of belief in a world of violence and deception. Writing from intimate acquaintance with Poe and with remarkable insight into the "pervading skepticism" of Poe's era, Sarah Helen Whitman compared the varieties of "unbelief" exhibited by such Romantics as De Quincey, Goethe, Byron, and Shelley and then delivered a trenchant observation about her onetime admirer: "Sadder, and lonelier, and more unbelieving than any of these, Edgar Poe came to sound the very depths of the abyss. The unrest and faithlessness of the age culminated in him. Nothing so solitary, nothing so hopeless, nothing so desolate as his spirit in its darker moods has been instanced in the literary history of the nineteenth century."[12]

If contemporary criticism has established, especially in Poe's poetry, an unflagging spiritual impulse, a preoccupation with transcendental experiences and supernal visions, it has also discerned in the fatality of his bleak tales a peculiarly modern "faithlessness," an inability to transcend his own hopelessly mortal condition. Torn between belief and doubt, Poe embodied the predicament of modernity in his alternately despairing materialism and desperate spirituality. This defining ambivalence frames the crisis of interpretation in *Pym* and suggests why modern readers recognize the urgency of Poe's fictional soundings of the abyss.

Notes and References

Chapter 2

1. See, for example, Grace Farrell Lee, "*Pym* and *Moby-Dick*," *American Transcendental Quarterly* 37 (Winter 1978): 73–86.

2. *The Knickerbocker* 13 (May 1839).

3. Letter to William E. Burton, 1 June 1840, *Letters of Edgar Allan Poe*, vol. 1, 130; Burton R. Pollin, "Poe's *Narrative of Arthur Gordon Pym* and the Contemporary Reviewers," *Studies in American Fiction* 2 (Spring 1974): 37–56.

4. W. H. Auden, "Introduction" to *Edgar Allan Poe: Selected Prose, Poetry, and Eureka*, ed. W. H. Auden (San Francisco: Rinehart, 1950), vii.

5. Edgar Allan Poe, review of *Robinson Crusoe*, *Southern Literary Messenger* (January 1836).

Chapter 3

1. Edgar Allan Poe, "Joseph Rodman Drake—Fitz-Greene Halleck," in *Edgar Allan Poe: Essays and Reviews*, ed. G. R. Thompson (New York: Library of America, 1984), 506.

2. Marie Bonaparte, *The Life and Works of Edgar Poe: A Psychoanalytic Interpretation*, trans. John Rodker (London: Imago, 1949).

3. Patrick F. Quinn, *The French Face of Edgar Poe* (Carbondale: Southern Illinois University Press, 1957), 176, 200.

4. Edward H. Davidson, *Poe: A Critical Study* (Cambridge: Harvard University Press, 1957), 161, 163, 169.

5. Harry Levin, *The Power of Blackness: Hawthorne, Melville, Poe* (New York: Alfred A. Knopf, 1958), 102, 123.

6. Leslie Fiedler, *Love and Death in the American Novel* (1960; rpt. New York: Dell, 1966), 393–94.

7. Sidney Kaplan, "Introduction" to *The Narrative of Arthur Gordon Pym* (New York: Hill and Wang, 1960), xxiii.

8. L. Moffitt Cecil, "The Two Narratives of Arthur Gordon Pym," *Texas Studies in Literature and Language* 5 (Summer 1963): 232–41.

9. Walter E. Bezanson, "The Troubled Sleep of Arthur Gordon Pym," in *Essays in Literary History*, ed. Rudolf Kirk and C. F. Main (New Brunswick, N.J.: Rutgers University Press, 1960), 151–52, 173.

10. J. V. Ridgely and Iola S. Haverstick, "Chartless Voyage: The Many Narratives of Arthur Gordon Pym," *Texas Studies in Literature and Language* 7 (Spring 1966): 80.

11. Sidney P. Moss, "*Arthur Gordon Pym*, or the Fallacy of Thematic Interpretation," *University Review* 33 (Summer 1967): 305.

12. Jean Ricardou, "Le Caractère singulier de cette eau," *Critique* 243–44 (August-September 1967): 729–30.

13. Joel Porte, *The Romance in America: Studies in Cooper, Poe, Hawthorne, Melville, and James* (Middletown, Conn.: Wesleyan University Press, 1969), 85–86, 90–91.

14. Joseph J. Moldenhauer, "Imagination and Perversity in *The Narrative of Arthur Gordon Pym*," *Texas Studies in Literature and Language* 13 (Summer 1971): 278.

15. Charles O'Donnell, "From Earth to Ether: Poe's Flight into Space," *PMLA* 77 (March 1962): 85–91.

16. Daniel Hoffman, *Poe, Poe, Poe, Poe, Poe, Poe, Poe* (Garden City, N.Y.: Doubleday, 1972), 271, 277.

17. Richard Wilbur, "Introduction to *The Narrative of Arthur Gordon Pym*," *Responses: Prose Pieces 1953–1973* (New York: Harcourt Brace Jovanovich, 1976), 193–94, 206, 214.

18. Todd M. Lieber, *Endless Experiments* (Columbus: Ohio State University Press, 1973), 188.

19. David Halliburton, *Edgar Allan Poe: A Phenomenological View* (Princeton, N.J.: Princeton University Press, 1973), 259, 267, 269.

20. Paul John Eakin, "Poe's Sense of an Ending," *American Literature* 45 (March 1973): 9–10, 14.

21. David Ketterer, *The Rationale of Deception in Poe* (Baton Rouge: Louisiana State University Press, 1979), 125–41.

22. G. R. Thompson, *Poe's Fiction: Romantic Irony in the Gothic Tales* (Madison: University of Wisconsin Press, 1973), 182.

23. Robert L. Carringer, "Circumscription of Space and the Form of Poe's *Arthur Gordon Pym*," *PMLA* 89 (May 1974): 512.

24. Claude Richard, "L'Ecriture d'Arthur Gordon Pym," *Delta* 1 (1975): 120–21.

Notes

25. J. Gerald Kennedy, "The 'Infernal Twoness' in *Arthur Gordon Pym*," *Topic* 30 (Fall 1976): 41–53.

26. John Carlos Rowe, "Writing and Truth in *The Narrative of Arthur Gordon Pym*," *Glyph* 2 (1977): 106.

27. William C. Spengemann, *The Adventurous Muse* (New Haven, Conn.: Yale University Press, 1977), 144, 48.

28. Alexander Hammond, "The Composition of *The Narrative of Arthur Gordon Pym*: Notes toward a Re-examination," *American Transcendental Quarterly* 37 (Winter 1978): 17.

29. Barton Levi St. Armand, "The Dragon and the Uroboros: Themes of Metamorphosis in *Arthur Gordon Pym*," *American Transcendental Quarterly* 37 (Winter 1978): 66.

30. Kent Ljungquist, "Descent of the Titans: The Sublime Riddle of *Arthur Gordon Pym*," *Southern Literary Journal* 10 (Spring 1978): 89.

31. John T. Irwin, *American Hieroglyphics: The Symbol of the Egyptian Hieroglyphics in the American Renaissance* (New Haven, Conn.: Yale University Press, 1980), 91, 117, 224, 235.

32. Paul Rosenzweig, "The Search for Identity: The Enclosure Motif in *The Narrative of Arthur Gordon Pym*," *ESQ* 26 (1980): 111–26.

33. Richard Kopley, "The Secret of *Arthur Gordon Pym*: The Text and the Source," *Studies in American Fiction* 8 (Autumn 1980): 209, 212–15.

34. Burton R. Pollin, "Introduction," in *The Imaginary Voyages*, vol. 1 (Boston: G. K. Hall, 1981), 9–12.

35. J. V. Ridgely, "The Growth of the Text," in Pollin, *Imaginary Voyages*, 29–36.

36. Douglas Robinson, "Reading Poe's Novel: *Pym* Criticism 1950–1980," *Poe Studies* 15 (1982): 47, 51.

37. John Carlos Rowe, *Through the Custom-House: Nineteenth-Century American Fiction and Modern Theory* (Baltimore: Johns Hopkins University Press, 1982); Richard Kopley, "The Hidden Journey of *Arthur Gordon Pym*," in *Studies in the American Renaissance 1982*, ed. Joel Myerson (Boston: Twayne, 1982), 29–51.

38. John Limon, "How to Place Poe's *Arthur Gordon Pym* in Science-Dominated Intellectual History and How to Extract It Again," *North Dakota Quarterly* 51 (Winter 1983): 41, 33.

39. Douglas Robinson, *American Apocalypses* (Baltimore: Johns Hopkins University Press, 1985), 120–21.

40. Richard Kopley, "The 'Very Profound Under-current' of *Arthur Gordon Pym*," in *Studies in the American Renaissance 1987*, ed. Joel Myerson (Charlottesville: University Press of Virginia, 1987), 157.

41. J. Gerald Kennedy, *Poe, Death, and the Life of Writing* (New Haven, Conn.: Yale University Press, 1987), 157, 148.

42. Dennis Pahl, *Architects of the Abyss: The Indeterminate Fictions of Poe, Hawthorne, and Melville* (Columbia: University of Missouri Press, 1989), 42.

43. John T. Irwin, "The Quincuncial Network of Poe's *Pym*," *Arizona Quarterly* 44 (Autumn 1988): 13–14.

44. G. R. Thompson, "Romantic Arabesque, Contemporary Theory, and Postmodernism: The Example of Poe's *Narrative*," *ESQ* 35 (1989): 263–69.

45. Cynthia Miecznikowski, "End(ings) and Mean(ings) in *Pym* and *Eureka*," *Studies in Short Fiction* 27 (Winter 1990): 61.

46. Lisa Gitelman, "*Arthur Gordon Pym* and the Novel Narrative of Edgar Allan Poe," *Nineteenth-Century Literature* 47 (December 1992): 355.

47. David Meakin, "Like Poles Attracting: Intertextual Magnetism in Poe, Verne, and Gracq," *Modern Language Review* 88 (July 1993): 607.

48. Jerome Loving, *Lost in the Custom House: Authorship in the American Renaissance* (Iowa City: University of Iowa Press, 1993), 55.

49. Dana Nelson, *The Word in Black and White: Reading "Race" in American Literature* (New York: Oxford University Press, 1992), 105.

50. Joan Dayan, "Romance and Race," in *The Columbia History of the American Novel*, ed. Emory Elliott (New York: Columbia University Press, 1991), 108–9.

51. John Carlos Rowe, "Poe, Antebellum Slavery, and Modern Criticism," in *Poe's "Pym": Critical Explorations*, ed. Richard Kopley (Durham, N.C.: Duke University Press, 1992), 118–27.

52. Susan Beegel, "'Mutiny and Atrocious Butchery': The *Globe* Mutiny as a Source for *Pym*," in Kopley, *Poe's "Pym*," 7–19; J. Lasley Dameron, "*Pym*'s Polar Episode: Conclusion or Beginning?" in ibid., 33–43; Joseph J. Moldenhauer, "Pym, Dighton Rock, and the Matter of Vinland," in ibid., 75–94.

53. Bruce I. Weiner, "Novels, Tales, and Problems of Form in *The Narrative of Arthur Gordon Pym*," in ibid., 56.

54. Grace Farrell, "Mourning in Poe's *Pym*," in ibid., 107–16.

55. Kenneth Silverman, *Edgar A. Poe: Mournful and Never-ending Remembrance* (New York: HarperCollins, 1991), 135–36.

56. David Hirsch, "'Post-Modern' or Post-Auschwitz: The Case of Poe," in Kopley, *Poe's "Pym*," 141–50; Alexander Hammond, "Consumption, Exchange, and the Literary Marketplace: From the Folio Club Tales to *Pym*," in ibid., 153–66; J. Gerald Kennedy, "*Pym* Pourri: Decomposing the Textual Body," in ibid., 167–74.

57. John Barth, "'Still Farther South': Some Notes on Poe's *Pym*," in ibid., 229–30.

Notes

58. David Ketterer, "Tracing Shadows: *Pym* Criticism 1980–1990, with Bibliography: A Checklist of *Pym* Criticism," in ibid., 235, 264.

Chapter 4

1. William Burton, review of *The Narrative of Arthur Gordon Pym*, by Edgar Allan Poe, *Gentleman's Magazine*, September 1838, n. pag.; cited by Pollin in "Poe's *Narrative*," 40.

2. Letter from Harper and Brothers, June 1836, cited in Quinn, *Poe: A Critical Biography*, 251.

3. Edgar Allan Poe, "Mystification," in *Collected Works of Edgar Allan Poe*, ed. Thomas Ollive Mabbott, vol. 2 (Cambridge: Harvard University Press, 1978), 303.

Chapter 5

1. This lack of planning also reveals itself in Pym's reference, at the end of the chapter, to the *Ariel* escapade and to his having subsequently "talked the matter over" (64) with Augustus. There is no hint here that Augustus will die in chapter 13, a mere six weeks into the voyage of the *Grampus*.

2. Richard Wilbur, "The Narrative of Arthur Gordon Pym," in *Responses: Prose Pieces 1953–1976* (New York: Harcourt Brace Jovanovich, 1976), 196. Wilbur noted some of the "personal references" tucked into the story but cautioned, "it is a waste of time to try to understand the characters of Poe's major fiction as so many real people with real-life originals and ordinary motives."

3. We must also keep in mind that someone—probably Thomas W. White—gave away the game by identifying Poe as the author when the first installment of the narrative appeared in the *Messenger*.

4. For example, Pym renders the rescue of Augustus in meticulous detail despite the fact that he has been lying unconscious in the ship's cabin during the entire operation.

5. Davidson, *Poe: A Critical Study*, 164.

6. Richard Wilbur, "Introduction to *Pym*," in *Responses*, 214.

7. Barth, "'Still Farther South,'" 229.

8. Mabbott, *Collected Works of Edgar Allan Poe*, vol. 2, 145.

Chapter 6

1. Moldenhauer, "Imagination and Perversity," 275.

2. Rowe, "Writing and Truth," 113.

3. Bezanson, "The Troubled Sleep of Arthur Gordon Pym," 152.

4. Poe shortly places this event in a more ironic perspective when Pym suddenly remembers, five days after the slaughter of Parker, the location of an ax, which leads to the recovery of food from the submerged hold.

5. Hoffman, *Poe Poe Poe*, 269.

Chapter 7

1. Pollin, *Imaginary Voyages*, 288–316. The discussion of sources and the notes for these chapters form the most complete accounting to date of Poe's borrowings. See also Kopley, *Poe's "Pym"*, 7–103, for additional sources.

2. See Kopley, "The Secret of *Arthur Gordon Pym*," 205–06; Irwin, "The Quincuncial Network," 1–14; and Thompson, "Romantic Arabesque," 163–292. As Pollin points out in *Imaginary Voyages* (292–97), when critics infer symbolic purposes on Poe's part, they must bear in mind that these paragraphs came from Morrell.

3. See Pollin's commentary on these references, *Imaginary Voyages*, 307–11.

Chapter 8

1. Sidney Kaplan, "Introduction" to *Pym* (1960), xv–xxv.

2. Dana Nelson, "Ethnocentrism Decentered: Colonialist Motives in *The Narrative of Arthur Gordon Pym*," in *The Word in Black and White: Reading 'Race' in American Literature* (New York: Oxford University Press, 1991), 90–108.

3. Readers may remember that during the countermutiny aboard the *Grampus*, Peters dispatched William Allen, who had been standing watch on the forecastle. This family name obviously recalls that of Poe's foster father—John Allan, who died in 1834—and perhaps implies the author's residual hostility toward him.

4. Poe used nearly the same language in his 1844 "bugaboo" tale, "The Premature Burial." For a more comprehensive discussion of Poe's fixation on living interment, see J. Gerald Kennedy, "Notes from Underground" in *Poe, Death, and the Life of Writing*, 32–59.

5. Acknowledging an error in the first edition of *Pym*, Pollin in *Imaginary Voyages* numbered this as chapter 23 bis; in other editions it appears simply as chapter 24.

6. Fiedler, *Love and Death*, 396.

Notes

Chapter 9

1. Pollin, *Imaginary Voyages*, 342.

2. Paul John Eakin positions his argument for a "complete" ending against the "unsparing" verdict of Henry James (in his introduction to *The Altar of the Dead*, New York Edition), who insisted that "the climax fails . . . , stops short for want of connexions." See Eakin, "Poe's Sense of an Ending," 1.

3. Pym makes these observations, we should note, while conceding that he cannot be accurate about dates and that he provides such details to enhance the "perspicuity of narration." By reminding us that the published account is based on Pym's "pencil memoranda" (203n), Poe calls attention to the process of writing and invites us to imagine how his narrator managed to keep any records.

4. Poe also used this idea in his 1833 tale "Ms. Found in a Bottle." For the possible influence of Symmes on *Pym*, see Pollin, *Imaginary Voyages*, 356.

5. Edgar Allan Poe, "Ms. Found in a Bottle," in Mabbott, *Collected Works of Edgar Allan Poe*, vol. 2, 145.

6. See Pollin, *Imaginary Voyages*, 356–59, for a summary of many readings of the shrouded figure, especially an 1838 account by Reynolds. See also Dameron, "*Pym*'s Polar Episode," 41–42, for findings of a "colossal" figure in the Scoresby material. See "*Pym*'s Polar Episode: Conclusion or Beginning?" in *Poe's "Pym"*, 41–42. John Irwin's case for the polar shadow appears in *American Hieroglyphics*, 205–23; and Richard Wilbur makes the case for a spiritual presence in *Responses*, 212.

7. See Robinson, *American Apocalypses*, 111–22.

8. Sigmund Freud, *Totem and Taboo*, trans. A. A. Brill (New York: Random House, 1946), 26.

Chapter 10

1. Hammond, "The Composition of *The Narrative*," 9–20.

2. Note, for example, that Wilbur (in the "Introduction" to *Pym* reprinted in *Responses*) avoided altogether the problem of the note; likewise, Eakin (in "Poe's Sense of an Ending") mentioned the addendum (15–16) but ignored its subversive implications.

3. See, for example, Pollin, *Imaginary Voyages*, 359, for a comment about a "dimly considered sequel."

4. See especially Kaplan, introduction to *The Narrative*, xx–xxv.

5. Ibid., xxiii.

6. See Dayan, "Romance and Race," 109. Such a reading, of course, assumes that Poe considered slavery evil or that he at least had misgivings about the institution.

7. Irwin, *American Hieroglyphics*, 227–30; Maurice Mourier, "Le tombeau d'Edgar Poe," *Esprit* 42 (December 1974): 916–20.

8. See the *Oxford English Dictionary*, s.v. "shady." The connotation of *shady* as 'dishonest' or 'disreputable' had become familiar enough by 1848 that the English poet Arthur Clough could so use it in a literary setting. It is at least possible that this connotation was available to Poe a decade earlier in America.

9. E. D. Hirsch, *Validity in Interpretation* (New Haven: Yale University Press, 1967), 74.

10. J. V. Ridgely, "Tragical-Mythical-Satirical-Hoaxical: Problems of Genre in *Pym*," *American Transcendental Quarterly* 24 (1974): 8.

11. Poe to James Kirke Paulding, 19 July 1838, *The Letters of Edgar Allan Poe*, ed. John Ward Ostrom, vol. 2 (New York: Gordian Press, 1966), 681.

12. Sarah Helen Whitman, *Edgar Poe and His Critics* (New York: Rudd and Carleton, 1859), 65.

Selected Bibliography

Primary Works

The Narrative of Arthur Gordon Pym of Nantucket. New York: Harper and Brothers, 1838.

The Narrative of Arthur Gordon Pym. In *The Imaginary Voyages*, vol. 1, edited by Burton R. Pollin, 1–363. Boston: Twayne Publishers, 1981.

Secondary Works

Bibliographies

Hyneman, Esther F. *Edgar Allan Poe: An Annotated Bibliography of Books and Articles in English, 1827–1973.* Boston: G. K. Hall, 1974. A comprehensive summary of Poe scholarship and criticism, including early reviews.

Ketterer, David. "Tracing Shadows: *Pym* Criticism 1980–1990, with Bibliography: A Checklist of *Pym* Criticism." In *Poe's "Pym": Critical Explorations*, edited by Richard Kopley, 233–74. Durham, N.C.: Duke University Press, 1992. An analytical review.

Robinson, Douglas. "Reading Poe's Novel: A Speculative Review of *Pym* Criticism, 1950–1980." *Poe Studies* 15 (1982): 47–54. Categorizes critical methods applied to *Pym*, the "interpreter's dream text," over three decades.

Books

Bonaparte, Marie. *The Life and Works of Edgar Allan Poe: A Psychoanalytic Interpretation*. Translated by John Rodker. London: Imago, 1949. A comprehensive Freudian analysis of symbolic patterns in Poe, including the search in *Pym* for the Mother.

Davidson, Edward H. *Poe: A Critical Study*. Cambridge, Mass.: Harvard University Press, 1957. Discusses *Pym* as a quest for knowledge and selfhood in a world of deception.

Fiedler, Leslie. *Love and Death in the American Novel*. New York: Dell Publishing Co., 1966. A provocative psychosymbolic reading that discusses male bonding and the flight from domesticity in Poe's novel.

Halliburton, David. *Edgar Allan Poe: A Phenomenological View*. Princeton, N.J.: Princeton University Press, 1973. Emphasizes the sensational, experiential aspects of Pym's spiritual quest.

Hoffman, Daniel. *Poe Poe Poe Poe Poe Poe Poe*. Garden City, N.Y.: Doubleday & Co., 1972. A lively exploration of Pym's "regressive imagination" in mythic and psychoanalytic terms.

Irwin, John T. *American Hieroglyphics: The Symbol of the Egyptian Hieroglyphics in the American Renaissance*. New Haven, Conn.: Yale University Press, 1980. An intricate deconstruction of *Pym* as a "symbolic quest for the origin of writing."

Kennedy, J. Gerald. *Poe, Death, and the Life of Writing*. New Haven, Conn.: Yale University Press, 1987. Links Pym's rehearsals for death to the interpretive problem of unreadability.

Ketterer, David. *The Rationale of Deception in Poe*. Baton Rouge: Louisiana State University Press, 1979. Maintains that Pym survives multiple deceptions to experience an "apocalyptic vision."

Kopley, Richard, ed. *Poe's "Pym": Critical Explorations*. Durham, N.C.: Duke University Press, 1992. Wide-ranging, diverse essays on sources, contexts, and textual patterns.

Levin, Harry. *The Power of Blackness: Hawthorne, Melville, Poe*. New York: Alfred A. Knopf, 1958. Discusses Poe's urge for the "subterranean" and the irrational.

Lieber, Todd M. *Endless Experiments*. Columbus: Ohio State University Press, 1973. Traces mythic patterns in the novel, especially Pym's quest for "pure selfhood."

Limon, John. *The Place of Fiction in the Time of Science: A Disciplinary History of American Writing*. New York: Cambridge University Press, 1990. Reframes the connections between *Pym* and *Eureka* posited in his 1983 essay.

Ljungquist, Kent. *The Grand and the Fair: Poe's Landscape Aesthetics and*

Pictorial Techniques. Potomac, Md.: Scripta Humanistica, 1984. Repeats his argument for the Titan myth as a source of "sublimity" in *Pym,* originally stated in his 1978 article "Descent of the Titans."

Loving, Jerome. *Lost in the Custom House: Authorship in the American Renaissance.* Iowa City: University of Iowa Press, 1993. Places *Pym* in the context of the American preoccupation with awakenings and new beginnings.

Nelson, Dana. *The Word in Black and White: Reading 'Race' in American Literature, 1638–1867.* New York: Oxford University Press, 1992. Sees Poe's treatment of race in *Pym* as a critique of cultural superiority and "colonial knowledge."

Pahl, Dennis. *Architects of the Abyss: The Indeterminate Fictions of Poe, Hawthorne, and Melville.* Columbia: University of Missouri Press, 1989. Examines the problem of authority in relation to the putative death of Pym as author.

Pease, Donald. *Visionary Compacts: American Renaissance Writings in Cultural Context.* Madison: University of Wisconsin Press, 1987. Reads *Pym* as a display of resistance to adventure and novelty, dismissing Poe's interest in exploration.

Porte, Joel. *The Romance in America: Studies in Cooper, Poe, Hawthorne, Melville, and James.* Middletown, Conn.: Wesleyan University Press, 1969. Discusses the novel as a journey toward "eternal terror," emphasizing Pym's self-deception.

Quinn, Patrick F. *The French Face of Edgar Poe.* Carbondale: Southern Illinois University Press, 1957. A landmark case for *Pym*'s centrality in the Poe canon, tracing the themes of revolt and deception.

Robinson, Douglas. *American Apocalypses.* Baltimore: Johns Hopkins University Press, 1985. Sees the ironies of *Pym*'s ending as a paradoxically visionary strategy.

Rowe, John Carlos. *Through the Custom-House: Nineteenth-Century American Fiction and Modern Theory.* Baltimore: Johns Hopkins University Press, 1982. Expands on his 1977 essay, deconstructing writing as the representation of truth in *Pym.*

Silverman, Kenneth. *Edgar A. Poe: Mournful and Never-ending Remembrance.* New York: HarperCollins, 1991. Contends that *Pym* "memorializes many dead figures in Poe's past."

Spengemann, William C. *The Adventurous Muse.* New Haven, Conn.: Yale University Press, 1977. Discusses Poe's "subversive manipulations" of travel-narrative conventions.

Thompson, G. R. *Poe's Fiction: Romantic Irony in the Gothic Tales.* Madison: University of Wisconsin Press, 1973. Relates mockery and reversal in *Pym* to romantic irony.

Veler, Richard P., ed. *Papers on Poe*. Springfield, Ohio: Chantry Music Press, 1972. A collection of essays on sundry topics, including *Pym*.

Articles

Auden, W. H. "Introduction" to *Edgar Allan Poe: Selected Prose, Poetry, and "Eureka"*, edited by W. H. Auden, vii. San Francisco: Rinehart, 1950. Considers *Pym* a great novel of adventure.

Bailey, J. O. "Sources of Poe's *The Narrative of Arthur Gordon Pym* and 'Hans Pfaal' and Other Pieces." *PMLA* 57 (1942): 513–35. An early but still useful source study.

Barth, John. "'Still Further South': Some Notes on Poe's *Pym*." In *Poe's "Pym": Critical Explorations*, edited by Richard Kopley, 217–30. Durham, N.C.: Duke University Press, 1992. Finds the novel occasionally brilliant but flawed and overrated.

Beegel, Susan. "'Mutiny and Atrocious Butchery': The *Globe* Mutiny as a Source for *Pym*." In *Poe's "Pym": Critical Explorations*, edited by Richard Kopley, 7–19. Durham, N.C.: Duke University Press, 1992. Considers Poe's possible knowledge of an 1824 mutiny.

Bezanson, Walter E. "The Troubled Sleep of Arthur Gordon Pym." In *Essays in Literary History*, edited by Rudolf Kirk and C. F. Main, 149–77. New Brunswick, N.J.: Rutgers University Press, 1960. An analysis of unconscious patterns in Poe's "dream book."

Carringer, Robert L. "Circumscription of Space and the Form of Poe's *Arthur Gordon Pym*." *PMLA* 89 (May 1974): 506–16. Sees *Pym* as inimical to Poe's preference for tight spots and closed forms.

Cecil, L. Moffitt. "Two Narratives of Arthur Gordon Pym." *Texas Studies in Literature and Language* 5 (Summer 1963): 232–41. A textual study rejecting the notion of *Pym* as a unified work.

Dameron, J. Lasley. "*Pym*'s Polar Episode: Conclusion or Beginning?" In *Poe's "Pym": Critical Explorations*, edited by Richard Kopley, 33–43. Durham, N.C.: Duke University Press, 1992. Argues that William Scoresby's journal lent realism to Poe's last chapter.

Dayan, Joan. "Romance and Race." In *The Columbia History of the American Novel*, edited by Emory Elliott, 107–09. New York: Columbia University Press, 1991. Makes the case that *Pym* depends on "a crisis of color."

Eakin, Paul John. "Poe's Sense of an Ending." *American Literature* 45 (March 1973): 1–22. Paradoxical, visionary reading of the "Lazarus theme" in Poe's novel.

Farrell, Grace. "Mourning in Poe's *Pym*." In *Poe's "Pym": Critical Explorations*, edited by Richard Kopley, 107–16. Durham, N.C.: Duke

University Press, 1992. Contends that death is central to this "novel of mourning."

Gitelman, Lisa. "Arthur Gordon Pym and the Novel Narrative of Edgar Allan Poe." *Nineteenth-Century Literature* 47 (December 1992): 349–61. Reads *Pym* as a mocking critique of the dull language and predictable materials in nineteenth-century accounts of exploration.

Hammond, Alexander. "The Composition of *The Narrative of Arthur Gordon Pym*: Notes toward a Re-Examination." *American Transcendental Quarterly* 37 (Winter 1978): 9–20. Develops a strong case that *Pym* was essentially completed by mid-1837.

———. "Consumption, Exchange, and the Literary Marketplace: From the Folio Club Tales to *Pym*." In *Poe's "Pym": Critical Explorations*, edited by Richard Kopley, 153–66. Durham, N.C.: Duke University Press, 1992. Reads the novel as an oblique, figurative commentary on Poe's literary situation.

Hinz, Evelyn J. "Tekeli-li: *The Narrative of Arthur Gordon Pym* as Satire." *Genre* 3 (1970): 379–97. Finds in *Pym* features of "Menippean satire," invoking Northrop Frye.

Hirsch, David. "'Post-Modern' or Post-Auschwitz: The Case of Poe." In *Poe's "Pym": Critical Explorations*, edited by Richard Kopley, 141–50. Durham, N.C.: Duke University Press, 1992. Argues that *Pym* prefigures the "dehumanized" vision of the Holocaust.

Irwin, John T. "The Quincuncial Network of Poe's *Pym*." *Arizona Quarterly* 44 (Autumn 1988): 1–14. Discovers in the quincunx pattern of *Pym*'s bird nests a diagrammatic representation for human knowledge.

Kaplan, Sidney. "Introduction" to *The Narrative of Arthur Gordon Pym* by Edgar Allan Poe, vii–xxv. American Century Series. New York: Hill and Wang, 1960. First important exploration of the racial allegory depicted on Tsalal.

Kennedy, J. Gerald. "The Preface as a Key to the Satire in *Pym*." *Studies in the Novel* 5 (Summer 1973): 191–96. Examines the multiple ironies of the preface.

———. "'The Infernal Twoness' in *Arthur Gordon Pym*." *Topic* 30 (Fall 1976): 41–53. Treats the paradoxical letter from Augustus as a key to Poe's own duplicity.

——— "*Pym* Pourri: Deconstructing the Textual Body." In *Poe's "Pym": Critical Explorations*, edited by Richard Kopley, 167–74. Durham, N.C.: Duke University Press, 1992. Examines scenes of decay in *Pym* through the lens of anthropological theory.

Kopley, Richard. "The Secret of *Arthur Gordon Pym*: The Text and the Source." *Studies in American Fiction* 8 (1980): 203–18. Claims that Poe's "shrouded figure" is the figurehead of the *Penguin*.

———. "The Hidden Journey of *Arthur Gordon Pym*." In *Studies in the American Renaissance 1982*, edited by Joel Myerson, 29–51. Boston: Twayne Publishers, 1982. Contends that the "shrouded figure" is associated with Poe's deceased brother and mother.

———. "The '*Very* Profound Under-current' of *Arthur Gordon Pym*." In *Studies in the American Renaissance 1987*, edited by Joel Myerson, 143–75. Charlottesville: University Press of Virginia, 1987. Argues that *Pym* allegorizes the "destruction of Jerusalem," and that the "shrouded figure" becomes Christ.

Lee, Grace Farrell. "*Pym* and *Moby-Dick*: Essential Connections." *American Transcendental Quarterly* 37 (Winter 1978): 73–86. Examines suggestive parallels and speculates on the influence of *Pym* on *Moby-Dick*.

Limon, John. "How to Place Poe's *Arthur Gordon Pym* in Science-Dominated Intellectual History and How to Extract It Again." *North Dakota Quarterly* 51 (Winter 1983): 31–47. Reads *Eureka* as a conscious critique of science in *Pym*.

Ljungquist, Kent. "Descent of the Titans: The Sublime Riddle of *Arthur Gordon Pym*." *Southern Literary Journal* 10 (Spring 1978): 75–92. Argues that Jacob Bryant's *Mythology* inspired Poe's use of the Titan myth for sublime effects in *Pym*.

———. "'Speculative Methodology' and the Titan Myth in Poe's *Pym* and Melville's *Pierre*." *The Sphinx* 4 (1985): 250–7. Posits further connections between Poe and Melville.

McKeithan, D. M. "Two Sources of Poe's *The Narrative of Arthur Gordon Pym*." *University of Texas Studies in English* 13 (1933): 116–37. Another pioneering source study.

Mead, Joan Tyler. "Poe's 'Manual of Seamanship.'" In *Poe's "Pym": Critical Explorations*, edited by Richard Kopley, 20–32. Durham, N.C.: Duke University Press, 1992. Finds sources for *Pym*'s digressions on "stowage" and "lying to."

Meakin, David. "Like Poles Attracting: Intertextual Magnetism in Poe, Verne, and Gracq." *Modern Language Review* 88 (July 1993): 600–11. Explores metaphors of irresistible attraction as they link three divergent texts.

Miecznikowski, Cynthia. "End(ing)s and Mean(ing)s in *Pym* and *Eureka*." *Studies in Short Fiction* 27 (Winter 1990): 55–64. Argues that *Eureka* provides an "apologia" for the breakdown of language in *Pym*.

Moldenhauer, J. J. "Imagination and Perversity in *The Narrative of Arthur Gordon Pym*." *Texas Studies in Literature and Language* 13 (Summer 1971): 267–80. Discusses how *Pym*'s "perverse" imagination produces deliverance through destruction.

———. "*Pym*, the Dighton Rock, and the Matter of Vinland." In *Poe's*

"Pym": Critical Explorations, edited by Richard Kopley, 75–94. Durham, N.C.: Duke University Press, 1992. Maintains that contemporary controversy about the Vikings and Dighton Rock influenced *Pym* and its hieroglyphics.

Moss, Sidney P. "*Arthur Gordon Pym*, or the Fallacy of Thematic Interpretation." *University Review* 33 (Summer 1967): 298–306. Contends that Poe spins two separate tales that contradict the notion of unity.

———. "Poe's Apocalyptic Vision." In *Papers on Poe*, edited by Richard P. Veler, 42–53. Springfield, Ohio: Chantry Music Press, 1972. Punctures the visionary reading of *Pym*.

Mourier, Maurice. "Le Tombeau d'Edgar Poe." *Esprit* 42 (December 1974): 902–26. Decodes the inscriptions on Tsalal to locate the author's signature.

O'Donnell, Charles. "From Earth to Ether: Poe's Flight into Space." *PMLA* 77 (March 1962): 85–91. Initiates visionary claims by emphasizing Pym's "unconscious longing for unity."

Pollin, Burton R. "Poe's *Narrative of Arthur Gordon Pym* and the Contemporary Reviewers." *Studies in American Fiction* 2 (Spring 1974): 37–56. Details the diversity of early responses to *Pym*.

———. "The Narrative of Benjamin Morrell: Out of the Bucket and into Poe's *Pym*." *Studies in American Fiction* 4 (Autumn 1976): 157–72. Investigates one of Poe's major sources.

Quinn, Patrick F. "Poe's Imaginary Voyage." *Hudson Review* 4 (Winter 1952): 562–85. Launches the modern reconsideration of *Pym*.

Ricardou, Jean. "Le Caractère singulier de cette eau." *Critique* 243–44 (August-September 1967): 718–33. Translated by Frank Towne as "The Singular Character of the Water." *Poe Studies* 9 (1976): 1–6. First essay to examine the novel as a metacommentary on writing.

Richard, Claude. "L'Ecriture d'Arthur Gordon Pym" (The Narrative of Arthur Gordon Pym). *Delta* 1 (1975): 95–124. A development of Ricardou's suggestive approach.

Ridgely J. V., and Iola S. Haverstick. "Chartless Voyage: The Many Narratives of Arthur Gordon Pym." *Texas Studies in Literature and Language* 7 (Spring 1966): 63–80. Examines *Pym*'s "patchwork" composition process and its uneven results.

Ridgely J. V. "The End of Pym and the Ending of *Pym*." In *Papers on Poe*, edited by Richard P. Veler, 104–12. Springfield, Ohio: Chantry Music Press, 1972. Extrapolates from inscriptions a prior polar exploration by white people.

———. "Tragical-Mythical-Satirical-Hoaxical: Problems of Genre in *Pym*."

American Transcendental Quarterly 24 (Fall 1974): 4–9. Summarizes interpretive problems rooted in generic uncertainty.

———. "The Growth of the Text." In *Imaginary Voyages*, edited by Burton R. Pollin, 29–36. Boston: Twayne Publishers, 1981. Reviews the novel's composition through a possible 1838 completion.

Rosenzweig, Paul. "The Search for Identity: The Enclosure Motif in *The Narrative of Arthur Gordon Pym*." *ESQ* 26 (1980): 111–26. Extends and redirects Carringer's argument.

———. "'Dust within the Rock': The Phantasm of Meaning in *The Narrative of Arthur Gordon Pym*." *Studies in the Novel* 14 (1982): 137–51. Claims that Poe perpetually frustrates the desire for meaning in *Pym*.

Rowe, John Carlos. "Writing and Truth in *The Narrative of Arthur Gordon Pym*." *Glyph* 2 (1977): 102–21. A full-scale deconstruction of writing as a representation of truth.

———. "Poe, Antebellum Slavery, and Modern Criticism." In *Poe's "Pym": Critical Explorations*, edited by Richard Kopley, 117–38. Durham, N.C.: Duke University Press, 1992. Indicts Poe for "racism" and modern critics for complicity.

Seelye, John. "Introduction" to *The Narrative of Arthur Gordon Pym, Benito Cereno and Related Writings*. New York: J. B. Lippincott Co., 1967. Examines the shortcomings of *Pym* in relation to *Moby-Dick*.

St. Armand, Barton Levi. "The Dragon and the Uroboros: Themes of Metamorphosis in *Arthur Gordon Pym*." *American Transcendental Quarterly* 37 (Winter 1978): 57–71. Provides mythic analogues to the transformations of Poe's narrator.

Thompson, G. R. "Romantic Arabesque, Contemporary Theory, and Postmodernism: The Example of Poe's *Narrative*." *ESQ* 35 (1989): 163–271. Argues that the quincunx design of the bird nests in *Pym* epitomizes a postmodern ambivalence between meaning and meaninglessness.

Weiner, Bruce I. "Novels, Tales, and Problems of Form in *The Narrative of Arthur Gordon Pym*." In *Poe's "Pym": Critical Explorations*, edited by Richard Kopley, 44–56. Durham, N.C.: Duke University Press, 1992. Sees *Pym* as a succession of "tales of effect."

Wilbur, Richard. "Introduction" to *The Narrative of Arthur Gordon Pym* by Edgar Allan Poe. Boston: Godine, 1973. Reprinted in *Responses: Prose Pieces 1953–1976* by Richard Wilbur, 190–214. New York: Harcourt Brace Jovanovich, 1976. An impressive Christian, visionary reading emphasizing Poe's concern for "redemption."

Index

Index

Limon, John, 22
Literary hoax, 12, 20, 22, 32, 35, 80
Ljungquist, Kent, 21
Loving, Jerome: *Lost in the Custom House*, 25

Mark Twain: *The Adventures of Huckleberry Finn*, 16
Maury, Matthew Fontaine, 9, 14
Meakin, David, 25
Meaning/meaninglessness, 12, 13, 17, 25, 39, 40, 73, 78
Melville, Herman: *Moby-Dick*, 10–11, 12
Metaphysical crisis, 11–12, 13, 23, 83
Metatextual readings, 17, 20, 25, 27
Miecznikowski, Cynthia, 25
Moldenhauer, Joseph J., 18, 27, 42
Morrell, Benjamin, 55; *The Narrative of Four Voyages* 25, 54
Moss, Sidney P., 17
Mourier, Maurice, 80
Mythic readings, 18, 21

Narrative of Arthur Gordon Pym, The, 3, 9, 81; *Ariel* episode, 23, 36–40, 41; autobiographical connections in, 37; deconstruction of, 20, 21, 23, 24–25, 27, 71, 72; documentary chapters, 52–56; editorial note, 16, 62, 76–80; French criticism of, 15, 17; *Grampus* episode, 38, 42–51, 52, 53, 82; and identity of narrator, 51, 56, 62; interpretations of, 15–28, 71–72, 73, 81; journal entries, 67–68, 70, 73–74, 91n3; misreadings by narrator in, 12, 20, 45, 58–60, 62, 69, 78; and *Moby-Dick*, 10–11,

16; neglect of, 11, 15; philosophical split in, 82–83; as potboiler, 32; preface, 31–35, 36, 75–76; providential intervention in, 13, 38–40, 48, 49–50, 63, 69, 71, 81–83; publication of, 9, 11, 14–15; racial implications in (*see* Race); revaluation of, 11, 15; sequel, possibility of, 76–77; "shrouded human figure" in, 12, 70–71, 73, 91n6; *Tsalal* episode, 16, 17, 18–19, 26, 57–66, 69, 73, 78, 79
Nat Turner Rebellion, 4, 61
National Bank, 4
Native Americans, 5–6
Nelson, Dana: *The Word in Black and White*, 26, 61
New Criticism, 15, 16, 18
New England Magazine, 7, 8
New Historicism, 26, 27
Nullification controversy, 4, 5

O'Donnell, Charles, 18

Pahl, Dennis, 24
Panic of 1837, 9, 15
Party system, rise of, 3
Paulding, James Kirke, 81
Periodical publishing, 6–7
Plagiarism, 14, 15
Poe, Edgar Allan, 81, 83; on American readers, 14, 33, 75; and death, 23, 80; and slavery, 16, 26; and *Southern Literary Messenger*, 5, 8, 14, 31–32, 79; and verisimilitude, 13; works cited: *Complete Works*, 11; *Eureka*, 20, 22, 23; "The Fall of the House of Usher," 42; "The Gold-Bug," 16; "The Journal of Julius Rodman," 6; "The Man of the Crowd," 72;

Index

The Author

J. Gerald Kennedy received his doctorate in American literature in 1973 from Duke University, where he was elected to Phi Beta Kappa. Since then, he has been a member of the English department at Louisiana State University and has frequently served as director of the LSU in Paris summer program. His published work on Poe includes numerous articles and essays as well as the influential book *Poe, Death, and the Life of Writing*, published by Yale University Press in 1987. His essay on Roland Barthes and autobiography was a 1982 Pushcart Prize selection. He is also the author of *Imagining Paris: Exile, Writing, and American Identity*, a revisionary study on the expatriate movement, published by Yale University Press in 1993. His edition of Poe's *The Narrative of Arthur Gordon Pym*, in the World's Classics series from Oxford University Press, appeared in 1994. Currently he is editing a collection of essays, *Modern American Short Story Sequences*, for Cambridge University Press.